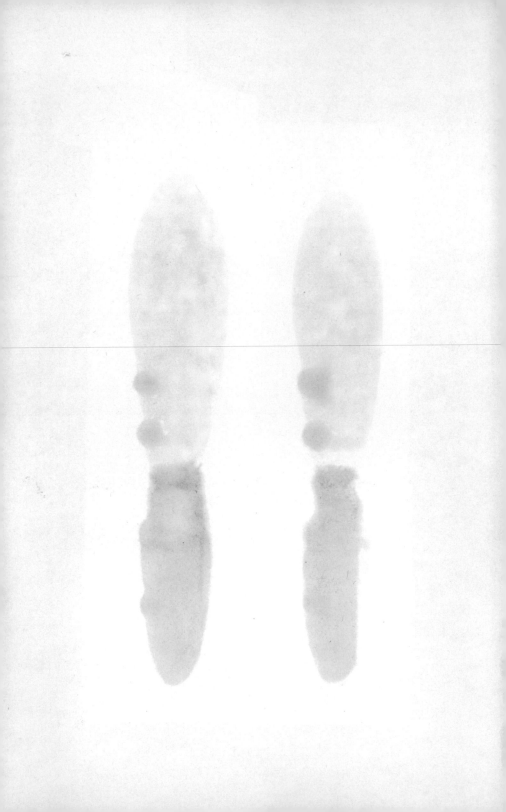

SIMON
and
GARFUNKEL

SIMON
and
GARFUNKEL

Robert Matthew-Walker

HIPPOCRENE BOOKS
New York

THE BATON PRESS

To Frank Welsh

784.5
S1moN

First published in 1984 by
THE BATON PRESS LTD
44 Holden Park Road,
Southborough, Tunbridge Wells

ISBN 0 85936 244 2 (UK)

First published USA in 1984 by
HIPPOCRENE BOOKS INC
171 Madison Avenue
New York, NY 10016

ISBN 0 88254 729 1 (USA)

Typeset by Studio.918
Printed in Great Britain by
Billings Limited, Worcester

Contents

Acknowledgements

This book could not have been written without the full-hearted co-operation of a number of people, and I would like to thank those who have helped at various stages. First, my friend Bob Stead, who set up the agreements under which it was written, and whose continuous support and encouragement during the occasionally trying circumstances that attended the completion of the manuscript were invaluable. My thanks are due also to Bob Giddings, who solved several practical problems, and to Graham Tuffery, who read and suggested many improvements to the original manuscript. My gratitude should also be extended to Geoffrey Cooper, who typed the manuscript with a selfless expertise that commanded my entire admiration.

Much practical assistance was rendered to me by Tony Woollcott of CBS Records, and by Peter Bailey when he was at Warner Bros. My old colleagues at CBS and long-standing friends in the rock music world deserve further thanks, for many kindnesses and illuminating discussions about Simon and Garfunkel going back several years. It would be invidious to omit them all or to mention them all, for the comments in this book that have not been acknowledged in the text are entirely mine, and no blame should be attached to these people for opinions expressed with which the reader might disagree.

Many of these people are probably unaware of the help they gave, but I must mention Dick Asher, Maurice Oberstein and the late Goddard Lieberson of CBS, and my other ex-colleagues James Fleming, Paddy Fleming, Andrew Pryor, Arthur Sheriff, Greg Edwards as well as the singer Ray Edwards, from all of whom I learned more than I could possibly say. Rodney Burbeck of *Music Week* and both Jack Florey and Derek Witt of CBS helped to sort out one or two problems in the final stages of the book. It would be unfair not to mention earlier books, by Spencer Leigh (whose *Paul Simon, Now and Then* remains a model of what books on rock musicians should be) and by Patrick Humphries (whose *Bookends* is a brilliantly researched and presented biography of the duo) from both of which I have gained a great deal.

These sources are sometimes acknowledged in the text, but not always so, as it has been felt on occasion more discreet to allow such comments to remain anonymous.

I have also to thank those associates of Midas Books – not all of whose advice I have followed – Ian Morley-Clarke, Liz Thomson and Candida Hunt for their suggestions and dedication to the task in hand, and finally the support extended to me by my wife, without which this book would never have seen the light of day.

The year given for the album before its discussion in the main body of the book is that of its first release. This rule is not rigidly adhered to when such a strict application of it would lead to albums being discussed out of sequence. The dates given in the discography are those of recording, not of release.

R.M.-W.
London.

1 Old Friends – *a biographical outline*

On Sunday 7 December 1941 at 1.25 p.m. EST over a hundred Japanese planes and a number of midget submarines attacked the US Pacific Fleet of eighty-six ships at anchor at Pearl Harbor, Hawaii. The US battleship *Arizona* was totally lost, and the battleships *Oklahoma, Nevada, California* and *West Virginia* were severely damaged together with eleven other ships. The US Navy lost eighty aircraft; the US Army ninety-seven. 2117 US naval officers and men were killed, with 960 missing and 876 wounded. Of the US Army, 226 officers and men were killed, and 396 were wounded.

A few hours later New York was buzzing with rumours. At Carnegie Hall the audience for that afternoon's orchestral concert by the Philharmonic Symphony Orchestra of New York under Artur Rodzinski were preparing to return to their seats after the intermission, in eager anticipation of the appearance by the pianist, Arthur Rubinstein. When conductor and soloist appeared, Rodzinski announced the news to a stunned audience. The gasps had hardly subsided before Rubinstein, sitting at the piano, spontaneously struck up 'The Star-spangled Banner'. Within seconds everyone in the auditorium had joined in the American National Anthem.

In Forest Hills, a suburb of Queens County, one of the five boroughs that make up the City of New York, a boy child was not forty-eight hours old at the time of the Japanese attack. He was Arthur Garfunkel, three weeks to the day younger than baby Paul Simon who had been born on 13 October in Newark, New Jersey. As young men their names would be inextricably linked.

They were members of what came to be known as the war generation – those children born during the conflict of the Second World War. They were not as directly affected by it as were children in Europe, but their lives were changed just the same by the powerful events of the period when they were born.

Both Simon and Garfunkel were, however, largely cushioned from the economic effects of the war in so far as they affected day-to-day life in New York City. Shortly after Paul Simon was born his parents moved to Forest Hills. His father was a teacher with a passion for music. Simon Senior played bass in several jazz combos, and his elder son soon exhibited a strong interest in music. (A second boy, Eddie, was born later.) By this time, according to some sources, Paul Simon had already met Art Garfunkel, though they were unable to communicate other than on a very basic level – through their mothers, who attended the same antenatal clinic. The Garfunkels were also enthusiastic musical amateurs, and in these congenial surroundings the boys were brought up to regard music as a necessary part of life, not as a dubious noisy pastime.

Simon's father also encouraged him to learn the guitar. The result of his thorough tuition on the instrument has been conclusively demonstrated on many of Paul Simon's later recordings. The boys, exact contemporaries, had much in common and went through school together. They were intelligent children, and were blessed with

10

parents who encouraged them. They shared mutual interests, principally music, though the eleven-year-old Art Garfunkel had appeared on stage for the first time in 1953 as the Cheshire cat in *Alice in Wonderland*. This was the time of Nat King Cole's massive hit song 'Too Young', and the young Simon and Garfunkel decided to perform it at their school concert. This was their first appearance together in public and it must have created a good impression, for within a short while the boys found themselves in demand at parties and barmitzvahs. They saw each other daily and their mutual interest in music (by no means their exclusive interest) was able to develop in a natural and effortless manner.

Already used to performing at local gigs, Simon and Garfunkel were naturally on the lookout for fresh material. Simon tried his hand at writing, and both avidly studied the Hit Parade charts. As their local fame grew, they adopted the stage names of Tom and Jerry. This wasn't after the Tom and Jerry of cartoon fame but two pseudonyms – Tom Graph (Garfunkel) and Jerry Landis (Simon). In 1957, when they were both fifteen, at a crucial stage in their development the Everly Brothers burst upon the international popular music scene with a succession of hits. They sang in flawless harmony, they were good guitarists and their lithe, clean sound and uncomplicated lyrics, together with their flawless presentation and winning good looks, soon made Simon and Garfunkel among their most ardent fans. Such classic cuts as 'Bye Bye Love' (one of only two Everly Brothers songs recorded by the mature Simon and Garfunkel) of the summer of 1957, 'Wake Up Little Susie' and 'All I Have To Do Is Dream' are full of typical Everly Brothers fingerprints of the time. The songs were nearly all similarly put together; for Simon and Garfunkel's purposes the best Everly Brothers manner was the breaking up of the songs into tiny phrases. These became clichés of late 1950s rock and roll, and clichés that abound in the Tom and Jerry first recordings. For a young duo on the make, the Everly Brothers' hits provided them with two priceless attributes: the quality of their material, which meant that just by copying them the young Simon and Garfunkel were learning excellent practical musicianship, and the success which meant that these songs were in popular demand.

Simon and Garfunkel decided to cut several acetates (what we would today call demo tapes). The succeeding story is pure Hollywood: the boys were 'discovered' by an influential producer at the studio, who soon had them signed to a company called Big Records. At the age of fifteen, therefore, Simon and Garfunkel made their first commercial recording. This was on the Big label: 'Hey Schoolgirl' became a notable hit in the USA, reportedly selling 100,000 copies as it made the US top forty.

The young duo made their first television appearance on the strength of their chance success on Thanksgiving Day in November 1957. Another Jerry was on the show (Dick Clark's *American Bandstand*), a more famous one – Jerry Lee Lewis, whose 'Great Balls of Fire' then stood at number one in the charts, and which, unlike the Tom and Jerry single, became a worldwide hit, reaching number one in Britain a few weeks later. But compared with the barely controlled outburst of Jerry Lee, which still has the power to shock and thrill a quarter of a century or more later, 'Hey Schoolgirl' is little more than a pleasantly inoffensive, not unattractive expression of high school puppy love. The singing is neat and tidy, and the performance has an attractive bounce. Paul Simon, who wrote it, evidently retains affection for this, his first hit. It is the earliest of his songs to be included in collections of his published music.

12

For all the giant figures of popular music whose success is both international and lasting, there are hundreds of 'one-hit' groups, whose talent – for a whole variety of reasons, the most common being bad luck – is unable to capitalize on the one hit they managed to achieve. It became a depressingly familiar formula for many American record companies: first get a hit, then carbon copy it for the follow-up, which almost invariably flops.

Tom and Jerry went the same way; their day in the sun, on this first outing, did not last, though several more singles were issued. Something happened to the Big label as well – the record company went bankrupt. No doubt prompted by growing parental concern, the one-hit pair returned to their school studies.

They were successful here as well; Garfunkel went to Columbia University to study mathematics and Simon to Queens University having chosen English literature. But the music bug had bitten deep and the effect was permanent. While at their respective universities in New York the pair naturally grew apart, though they still kept in touch, retaining their extra-curricular passion for music. Paul capitalized on his talent by making demo recordings of other writers' songs for 15 dollars a time. Burt Bacharach was an early customer, and Simon's earning power was increased when he sang the lead on another US hit, 'Motorcycle', temporarily becoming part of the group Tico and the Triumphs. This sold another 100,000, but flopped in Britain. He also sang lead on a Mystics single, 'Don't Tell the Stars', which flopped badly everywhere.

While at Queens, Simon met a fellow student, Carole Klein, who also wrote songs. Carole played piano and drums on many of Paul's demos, the pair calling themselves for this purpose 'The Cosines' (a reference to Garfunkel's mathematical status?). One of her songs they

13

put down as a demo tape, 'Just To Be With You', was taken up by the American group The Passions, who had a sizeable success with it. This success determined Carole to leave Queens and become a fulltime songwriter. Such a move was fraught with danger, and the circumspect Paul Simon advised her against such a course. She ignored his advice and within a year of leaving university had written ten hits with her co-writer, Gerry Goffin, including such classics as Bobby Vee's 'Take Good Care Of My Baby' and the Shirelles 'Will You Love Me Tomorrow?'. Her own voice is part of the pop culture of the time, for she had a big hit with her own single 'It Might As Well Rain Until September'.

For Paul Simon there was no success as yet, and he continued his studies by day and his music by night. The demands of study were proving more difficult as Simon realized where his heart lay. He left Queens and enrolled in law school. Arthur Garfunkel had also found that his studies did not meet all his requirements. Under the name of Artie Garr he made several singles for the (American) Warwick and Octavia labels. This was in 1961-2, and although the experience was invaluable none of the records made any impact. The pair remained in touch, more so when they returned as Tom and Jerry late in 1962 and cut their last single under this name, 'Lookin' at Me'. This was actually released in England in May 1963. This was a crucial time for Simon; he was twenty-one, and doubtless felt that he had something to contribute to popular music which was continually being frustrated by his studies. He left law school and worked on the fringe of the music business, plugging songs for a New York publisher.

Arthur Garfunkel had also left university, and their parallel ambitions naturally found an outlet in the burgeoning clubs of New York's Greenwich Village. For want of a better word 'folk' was the label attached to just about any singer whose guitar was not electric, and the label quickly became sanctioned whether the music was folk or not. Whatever it was, it was music, and was the natural expression of a part of Simon and Garfunkel's generation that was on the verge of making an original and significant contribution to popular culture. The man who personified this movement (indeed, for many people he *was* the movement) was Bob Dylan, a curious, enigmatic character with a burning but flawed vision. Like Simon and Garfunkel and many others, he played the Greenwich Village clubs and was discovered there by the legendary John Hammond of CBS Records. Hammond was one of the greatest record men the world has seen, for decades possessing an instinctive feel for quality music of all kinds. He had a quietly attractive, somewhat renegade personality which endeared him to many who met him, and eventually signed Dylan to the CBS label. The success of Dylan's first album astonished CBS; once again John Hammond was proved right. Suddenly record companies were on the lookout for more of the same. It was successful, and very cheap to record; one just put a singer with his acoustic guitar in front of a primitive pair of stereo microphones, started the tape machine, said 'Take one' and let him do it. Any resultant rough edges were part of the new style.

CBS had also lost heavily in the rock explosion of the middle to late 1950s, having virtually no answer to Elvis Presley, Buddy Holly, Little Richard, Gene Vincent, Jerry Lee Lewis, Bill Haley, the Everly Brothers and so on. They were anxious to break into the lucrative rock market and were also conscious of their 'respectable' image.

In the late spring of 1964 Simon planned a trip to England. The Beatles and the whole Mersey sound was at

15

the zenith of its early breakthrough and was poised to make giant inroads into the American market. For Paul Simon a visit to England was obligatory. He worked all over Britain playing solo gigs in small folk clubs and pubs and gaining much experience in the process.

CBS's product was distributed in England, at least until 1964-5, by Philips. The American giant wanted to set up independently in Britain, and did so by the effectively simple process of buying an existing small record company with its own plant. They chose Oriole Records, and it was from this small beginning that the British company grew to its present size. It could not have done this, of course, without the phenomenally successful range of artists it signed during the 1960s, including Simon and Garfunkel; but it was a happy coincidence that led Paul Simon to record a single for Oriole in London in 1964 under the pseudonym of Jerry Landis. He used another name – Paul Kane – as the writer. The songs were 'He Was My Brother' and 'Carlos Dominguez'. Garfunkel was also in Europe vacationing in Paris, and arranged to join his friend in London for a few days before returning with him to New York. It was a fateful step.

On their last night in London they went to the Flamingo Club in Soho's Wardour Street. The Ian Campbell folk group (early English performers of Dylan's songs) were due to perform but were unable to, and, as Judith Piepe recalled to Roy Carr of the *New Musical Express* in 1970,

There wasn't anyone around to entertain the large audience. Then suddenly we noticed a young kid with a guitar sitting on the floor. Curly Goss, the promoter, asked him his name. It was Paul . . . Paul Simon and he was American. Anyway, this unknown kid from New York was dragged onto the stage and started with 'Church Is Burning', followed it with 'Leaves That

16

Are Green' and then 'The Sound Of Silence'. Just then he waved to a tall fair-haired kid at the back of the club, asking him to join him and together they sang 'Benedictus'. Everyone was flabbergasted. They'd knocked the audience out. We got into conversation and soon learnt to our disappointment that both were returning to New York the next day.

This was the turning point. Simon and Garfunkel were in London because New York City had turned its back on them; they could not get work in their home town. The Flamingo appearance must have convinced them that they had been right all along. There is nothing more thrilling to a creative musician than to experience for himself the enthusiastic reception of his work by an audience. Judith Piepe was totally convinced by their performance, and after their return to the USA set to work on their behalf. Paul Simon returned to London at her invitation and appeared with Long John Baldry and even performed at the Edinburgh Folk Festival of 1964. At Judith Peipe's insistence he did a BBC session. With the growing confidence that comes from such certain live success, on his return to New York Simon approached Tom Wilson, the producer of Dylan's early recordings at the CBS offices there, and found a sympathetic ear. The result was Simon and Garfunkel's first CBS album, *Wednesday Morning, 3 a.m.*

It was not the instantaneous success everyone had hoped for, which was probably the main reason why the fledgling UK CBS company did not issue it immediately. In England Judith Piepe badgered the BBC to broadcast the material they had, and eventually succeeded. The religious themes running through several of Simon's early songs made them suitable for broadcasting in a daily five-minute religious spot called *Five to Ten* (in the morning). She also approached Reginald Warburton, a quiet, thoughtful man and first-class musician, an Oriole producer of wide experience, who was among the staff retained by CBS. He agreed to record an album of Paul Simon's songs, and encouraged by Miss Piepe's news Simon returned to England for the recording. The resulting *Paul Simon Songbook* is beautifully recorded and effectively simple, with Simon alone accompanying himself on his guitar. Simon's own liner notes are embarrassingly simple.

To promote the album he appeared all over the country, and Garfunkel joined him during the summer vacation in England. They gave a few gigs together, appeared on Independent Television and at Brixton Prison in South London among other places.

Simon, with the album under his belt, was beginning to make some headway in England. He co-wrote several songs for The Seekers (an immensely successful group in Britain, originally from Australia) and produced and part financed an EMI album in London for the American folk singer Jackson C. Frank.

However, back in New York things were also happening. On the West Coast a dealer had noted the interest of campus students in 'The Sounds Of Silence', which closes their début album, and suggested to his CBS rep that it should be issued as a single. The rep passed the suggestion to head office, and like all suggestions for material received by this company it was considered. Tom Wilson, having seen the recent transcontinental success of Dylan's 'Like a Rollin' Stone', decided – without reference to either Simon or Garfunkel – to add twelve-string guitar, bass and drums to the track, turning it into an example of the then fashionable 'folk rock'.

The result in commercial terms was a huge success; the single struck home without Simon's or Garfunkel's knowledge or participation, eventually reaching number

18

one in the US charts. In artistic terms it is a disaster, but it sold in vast quantities and after this things could never be the same again. It was covered in the UK by the Irish singers The Bachelors and reached number three. 'Homeward Bound' was issued as the follow-up in the USA, reaching the top ten there in March 1966 and number nine in Britain in April.

A new album became an urgent necessity, and the resultant *Sounds Of Silence* shows signs of hasty preparation. Only a few of the songs were new and some had been recorded by Paul Simon three times. By this time the duo was established in both America and Europe, and with such success their next album, also issued in 1966, was properly prepared. It is *Parsley, Sage, Rosemary and Thyme* and contains one of their most famous recordings, 'Scarborough Fair'. This was another notable success, but the album that did more to make them household names was one that in artistic terms is their least important. In 1967 the film of Charles Webb's novel *The Graduate* was made, and the following year was released by United Artists. Starring Anne Bancroft and Dustin Hoffman and directed by Michael Nicholls, it had songs by Paul Simon with additional music by David Grusin. The only new song was 'Mrs Robinson' (Anne Bancroft) but the album was fleshed out with Grusin's orchestral music and several earlier recordings by Simon and Garfunkel, though it does contain a previously unreleased version of 'The Sounds Of Silence'.

The film was a huge international commercial success and the millions who saw it also heard the music. The impact on the record sales of Simon and Garfunkel albums was enormous, and a new album, *Bookends,* was released at the same time as the film album. On 15 June 1968 'Mrs Robinson' was number one in the US singles chart, and in the album chart *The Graduate* was number one, *Bookends* was number two and *Parsley, Sage, Rosemary and Thyme* was number three. 'The Sounds Of Silence' stood at twenty-seven in the singles chart. This was the apogee of their popular commercial success – it seemed that nothing could cap this. However, their next album, effectively their last, was destined to become one of the three biggest selling albums in recorded history, with over 10 million copies sold worldwide.

Bridge Over Troubled Water took more than a year to make and was issued towards the end of 1969. It was their swan song. Following the success of *The Graduate* album and film Simon was swamped with offers to write film music. He declined them all, but Garfunkel was signed by Mike Nicholls to appear in his next film, *Catch 22*. As Simon said,

At the time of recording, we both had it in our minds that this would be be the last one together. What I think we actually said was something to the effect that we'll finish the album and that will be it. We hadn't any plan to do anything together after that. I planned to do an album by myself, and Artie went off to commence filming on the set of *Carnal Knowledge*. First off, the reason why Artie and I stopped touring was simple. We had both agreed that we had reached a logical conclusion to our constantly going out on the road. You've got to remember that we were locked into the same material each and every night. We were obligated to sing the required Simon and Garfunkel hits, which realistically speaking the audiences had come along to hear. I mean, we just couldn't say: 'I can't sing "Bridge Over Troubled Water" again because we've sung it so many times.' People want to hear it, and if you're going out on stage you've got to give the public what it wants. Therefore, when you are in that situation there are a lot of pressures forced on an act. So it was the logical end to the act. Also, having a track record to live up to and a string of success- ful records eventually becomes a hindrance. It becomes increasingly difficult to break away from what people naturally expect from you. From this point of view, I'm delighted that I didn't have to write a Simon and Garfunkel follow-up to 'Bridge Over Troubled Water' for, to be honest, I think that it would have been a let-down for everyone concerned.

Garfunkel's acting career continued with *Carnal Knowledge* in 1971, but this was his last film for eight years until he appeared in *Bad Timing* in 1980. His absence from the screen for such a long time was regrettable for he possesses genuine acting talent. However, during these years he issued four solo albums at approximately two-yearly intervals, and a fifth in 1981. Simon had married in 1969 and his son, Harper, was born the following year. Without an extra-musical career to pursue Simon concentrated on his solo albums and his writing. He issued a new album every year from 1972 to 1975, but his divorce in 1975 coincided with a slowing up of his output and a change of direction. Since then he has issued two records, the first the 'Greatest Hits' compilation for CBS (which contains two new songs) and the second a collection of songs for his own film, his *magnum opus, One-Trick Pony*, which appeared in 1980.

The film had occupied him on and off for a very long time. He wrote and starred in this compassionate film about a rock and roll singer. Although it has many fine qualities the film was not a success, and the songs from it lack the conviction of the best of his earlier work.

And so it would appear that these two had gone their separate ways more or less permanently. However, on 19 September 1981 they were reunited in the famous Concert in Central Park, when half a million New Yorkers turned out to see the first public reunion of this legendary duo for over a decade. It is clear that their

21

careers have reached a stage where it is possible to look back and examine the nature of their success. With this in mind, let us now turn our attention to the recorded legacy of Simon and Garfunkel.

2 Simon and Garfunkel recordings 1957 to 1966

1957

SIMON AND GARFUNKEL
(UK title when released in 1967; recorded by Simon and Garfunkel as TOM AND JERRY mainly in 1957)
For track listings see Discography p. 147

This album, the first by Simon and Garfunkel and recorded when they were only fifteen, was of course not planned as such, and consists of a collection of singles put together after their later success. Although it was quickly withdrawn from sale when an injunction was served (it was packaged as though it was the latest offering from Simon and Garfunkel in 1967), it is not by any means hopeless and the young voices have an urgency and enthusiasm that were not always recaptured by the maturer men they became. It is redolent of high school bop music of the late 1950s, the kind of atmosphere made familiar to later generations by the success of the American television series, *Happy Days*. With this in mind and without looking for straws in a future wind each track deserves brief comment. 'Hey Schoolgirl', which opens the disc, was a minor hit in 1957, and is an attractive little boppy number, a baby driver with some nice chord changes not unworthy of the mature

23

composer. The Everly Brothers are to the fore in 'Our Song' (which happens to be record 24 on the local juke box). However, could not this 'song' of 'ours' be an old Everly Brothers hit? 'That's My Story' is well described by Spencer Leigh: the song 'owes something' to Neil Sedaka's 'Moon of Gold', an early Sedaka number, and although the title of the next song, 'Teenage Fool' is enough to make one cringe with embarrassment, it is not without a certain charm and some nice harmony, even if a little crude. The first side ends with 'Tiajuana Blues', an instrumental solo. It is a little cliché-ridden but it is quite well played. 'Dancin' Wild' was the follow-up to 'Hey Schoolgirl'. Like most follow-ups of the time it was a faded copy of the original. 'Don't Say Goodbye' and 'Two Teenagers' are further aspects of high school bop. The unrequited love of the first becomes an indulgent smile in the other, but neither track should be listened to with indulgence. 'True or False' concludes the proceedings for the singers with another piece of peppermint hokum before Paul Simon tackles 'Simon Says'. As it is an instrumental number, of course, he doesn't say.

1964

WEDNESDAY MORNING, 3 A.M.
For track listings see Discography p. 148

Hindsight is without doubt the best vantage point from which to view any event, but it is nevertheless difficult to understand the early decision by CBS in Great Britain not to release this album when it became available from America but to wait until October 1968 before doing so, by which time, of course, the importance of Simon and Garfunkel was apparent to anyone. It is not a flawless

24

album in layout, choice of repertoire or even performance, but it is still, after twenty years, immensely impressive, and contains some remarkable moments that retain the impact and fascination of surprise no matter how familiar the material has become. On the surface it is little more than a collection of songs of the time: cover versions of hits by other artists, 'recreative' attempts at material by other composers and – most important in the light of future developments – a selection of original songs by Paul Simon. This last ingredient ought to concern us the most, but in context all the performances demand detailed discussion. Beneath the surface there are more important happenings afoot, which will only gradually become clear as we go through the album in its published order.

'You Can Tell The World' is an unusual, because disappointing, beginning to the album – and, be it remembered, to the international recording career of these artists. The song is hardly guaranteed to set the world on fire even though the duo do everything they can for it. It is very fast with some fascinating quick-change chords, but the best 'hook' in it – the refrain 'Joy, joy, joy' – demonstrates their clear harmonic singing of the highest quality. The song's religious message – it is a revivalist-type number – is reminiscent of two important American groups of the early 1960s, the Everly Brothers (naturally enough, but only through the harmony) and the Kingston Trio. Nowhere else in the English-speaking world could such a fundamentalist religious message be expressed within a basically pseudo fervour. West Virginia is not far away, but in the next song, 'Last Night', we are further south in the Appalachian mountains, and the Kingston Trio (who had a hit with this very number) are not so much recalled as used as a starting point for an individual treatment of what is, again, not top-drawer material. The Vietnam War was the merest cloud on the horizon when this album was recorded, though when it was eventually released in Britain in 1968 it had become the most important and horrifying conflict since the Second World War. Consequently this is a peace song without much fervour, the only shocking event of comparable importance being President Kennedy's assassination the previous 22 November. The use of fingerpicking banjo reinforces the Southern atmosphere (which may be a subtle reference to the fact that the President had been assassinated in Dallas, Texas), but it confines the universal message to too local a geography. Because of this the song fails, but one should note its 3/4 beat (in four-bar phrases, a typical 'country' style of writing, producing in effect one massive bar of four beats) and the banjo triplets against the 3/4, which produces a tightening effect, the result being most imaginative. The coda is another miscalculation, being too short and unbalancing the song in the process.

With 'Bleecker Street' there is a sudden change of atmosphere: we hear the first song by Paul Simon on a mature Simon and Garfunkel album, and the effect is startling. The 'observer' appears.

Bleecker Street in New York City is a famous urban street containing those aspects of city life that often provide children with their initial vivid memories of the outside world and their upbringing. It is residential, with long tenement blocks that – in spite of rebuilding – retain their air of late nineteenth-century quasi slum. But it has a vibrant street life of its own, with stores and street traders and that incessant human activity that gives such places their own character. Every city has such streets; in London, perhaps the Portobello Road or Ladbroke Grove or even Deptford High Street or Camden Town come closest. Curiously enough, in the early 1950s the

Italian–American composer Gian-Carlo Menotti wrote an impressive modern-day three-act opera called *The Saint of Bleecker Street* for NBC television, which was concerned with the Italian working-class section of its inhabitants and their strong religious belief. One says curiously because with this song the underlying nature of the album – a fascination with aspects of religion – becomes much more pertinent and relevant. For example, the words are shot through with religious overtones – the references to the sacrament, church bells, and the fog rolling in from the East River bank which is likened to a shroud. But at the same time there is a chill in the air – the time is pre-dawn, just before the sun rises, with stillness and vast quiet movement, yet it is not inhuman. The reference to the sad café sums up in two words the pity of the observer of both the night shift worker and his unsocial hours, and the homeless street crawler whose hours are never social.

This masterly song is simply constructed. The harmonies are unsensational, yet the text for which they are used makes them new and original. Simon has the good sense to give lots of short instrumental breaks, mostly of just one bar, which fulfils a double purpose: a practical one for the singers to take a breather, and a subtler one to give the listener time to pause on the cryptic epigrams that run through the text like a gossamer thread. Clearly the poet here assumes considerable importance, a point not lost on Art Garfunkel's surprising notes on the sleeve. These have been described as pretentious, and while they may have seemed so at the time, a rereading of them confirms that Garfunkel knew perfectly well that what his partner had created was of considerable significance in popular music and was not afraid to say so. One senses this personal involvement in the performance, for (on the left-hand channel)

27

Garfunkel's voice is quite different in timbre from the first two songs, being deeper and more integrated with Simon's.

'Sparrow', which follows 'Bleecker Street', is also by Simon, but after the vivid imagery of the previous song this one is more direct and more restrained, though with this composer nothing can be taken for granted. The little bird is rejected by a succession of non-human images, which cumulatively suggest the plight of the world's hungry people. It may be coincidence, but the Indian politician Shastri (who died shortly after bringing together and signing the peace treaty of Tashkent), was known as the 'Sparrow' on account of his diminutive stature and his Gandhi-like self-denial; but the religious background, running like a deeper river of irrigation through this album, is based on Christian teaching. The Sermon on the Mount is recalled, not only in the plight of the hungry but also directly – consider the birds of the air – until finally the earth itself is returned from dust to dust. This wholly remarkable song works, therefore, on several levels and one can understand the composer's sense of frustration at the neglect of his work, even by the overseas branches of his record company. 'Bleecker Street' and 'Sparrow' (to say nothing of several others on the album, which came later) are so far in advance of just about anything else that was appearing in popular music in 1964 that one does not need hindsight to realize that the career of this pair hung on a thread at the time. One very small point: Garfunkel is late with his very first entry – not a major flaw by any means, but one which in later years would have been retaken and edited out to produce a flawless performance. It is difficult not to feel that the inclusion of this faulty take actually enhances the sense of real music-making. 'The letter killeth: but the spirit giveth life.'

28

If 'Bleecker Street' and 'Sparrow' are much more potent than the somewhat bland opening songs, the next track, 'Benedictus', is astonishing. We have long since become used to hearing bits of the classics being taken up to make hit songs when a writer is so bereft of ideas that he has to take someone else's, but the composer concerned is usually famous – Bach, Beethoven, Tchaikovsky, *et al.* 'Benedictus' is many things on this album – the first is that it throws the religious theme of the album into sharp relief, for the Benedictus, In Nomine Domine, is taken from the ordinary of the Latin Mass. The second is that the setting is a genuine sixteenth-century one by an anonymous composer that Garfunkel had come across in a New York library. It follows, therefore, that this is a sincere and legitimate performance of a piece of sixteenth-century European polyphony. It is as well to point out that a cello is discreetly added to the texture, which is not so objectionable to classical purists as might at first appear. At the time this music first saw the light of day organs in churches were very primitive affairs – remember this is 150 years before the birth of J. S. Bach, and the use of stringed instruments was by no means universally discouraged in worship. Although many people might term this 'classical' music in strict terms it is 'pre-classical', i.e. before about the mid-seventeenth century, and this 'early music' (as it is now generally known) was at the time of Simon and Garfunkel's amazing decision to include this on their début album of the greatest interest in New York's cultural and musical life. No resident of Greenwich Village, or indeed anyone who regarded himself as being on at least nodding acquaintance with the artistic life of the city, could remain unaware of the work of the New York Pro Musica Antiqua and their inspired founder and director, Noah Greenberg. They made over a dozen albums that had enormous world-wide sales and impact on other musicians, and some of the most respected names in the performance of early music, perhaps most notably James Tyler, played with Greenberg. The Riverside Chamber Singers, another New York ensemble, had a similar impact, and this track created a sensation among rock musicians in England when the album finally appeared late in 1968.

In spite of the enormous risk involved, the performance of this haunting Benedictus fragment is very fine indeed. The phrasing and harmony singing would do justice to any classically trained duo, and the result is a remarkable achievement to which no true lover of early music could possibly object.

As if these three songs were not enough to set people talking, the side ends with the quintessential Simon and Garfunkel song making its first appearance on disc – 'The Sounds Of Silence'. Apart from being, as Garfunkel correctly, if a trifle pretentiously, says in his sleeve note, 'a major work', and in the fullness of time a classic song, it continues the themes of the album, albeit at a distance. The religious aspect is less clear, but it is there: the words 'halo', 'prayed' and the phrase 'voices of the prophets' demonstrate this positively, but other undercurrent themes, of night and of dreams, which also run through this album, are there as well. Before discussing this song it is perhaps pertinent to comment on the two ways in which the title is listed – 'The Sound Of Silence' and 'The Sounds Of Silence'. CBS are unsure, for the song is listed one way on the sleeve and another way on the label, a confusion reinforced in *The Paul Simon Songbook*, which titles the piece 'The Sound Of Silence' but in the text prints 'Sounds'. Which is right, and does it matter? Curiously enough, an examination of the performances reveals that both are correct, and the confusion stems from this first recording: Simon sings 'sounds' while at the same time Garfunkel sings 'sound'. It matters because Simon is a fastidious artist with a profound understanding of the English language, to whom the tiniest detail is significant. For that reason, Art Garfunkel notwithstanding, it is probably better to follow the composer, who sings 'The Sounds Of Silence'.

The song begins quietly, moderately, with a single bar of unaccompanied guitar tracery oscillating between three notes; the singers' entry has Garfunkel with the melody and Simon providing the harmony. The result is an ethereal texture, like a faintly glowing object in the sky (Garfunkel) with the worldly shadows darkening the earth below (Simon). The sense of ebb and flow is achieved by the simplest means: the song is basically broken up into two-bar phrases, the first being of quavers (quarter-notes) and the second of minims (four or eight times as long). During the second bar of each phrase the guitar repeats the even quavers of the previous bar, the whole thing moving with the certainty of the lunar tide. This first verse is held at the same even tenor, but the second and third show a marked increase in intensity, as the 'observer' of Bleecker Street is himself affected by the soulless existence of much contemporary life. Simon himself must have felt conscious of the line 'People writing songs that voices never share' in regard to his own work at this time, but with the fourth verse (the penultimate) the additional guitars of the second and third verses are abandoned and the accompaniment returns to the instrumentation of the opening, against Simon's voice in the harmony becoming clearly much more aggressive as he emphasizes his own ' "Fools," said I, "You do not know, silence like a cancer grows." ' The music is loud now, the loudness of emphasis and certainty, not of strident self-aggrandizement. The phrases 'subway walls' and 'tenement halls' refer again to Bleecker Street and to the contemporary nature of the underlying themes of the album; and then, with great daring, Simon ends his song quite suddenly. But this time there is no shock of being cut off too soon; the message is so powerful and immediate that its very restraint makes it the more potent, and the single guitar that ushered in this masterpiece now reappears to carry it gently on its way. The final chord, too, is surprising, for although the song is in D minor and remains so throughout (which has the effect of concentrating the listener's attention on the words) the note that confirms D minor – F natural – is completely absent from the final chord. We are left with a bare fifth; almost unheard of in a popular song, but common musical parlance in pre-classical music of the sixteenth century and earlier. In such tiny matters are the subtlety and intelligence of these two musicians revealed, for such a point echoes the Benedictus.

So ends the first side of this first album, and at this point one might well pause to ask again why it was not released at the earlier time. As must be clear to even the most cursory reader, this first side has grown beyond all expectation; but it must be confessed that the second side does not sustain this level of achievement. It is a disappointment and seems at one point to be content to go through the motions we have already heard on side one. 'He Was My Brother', which opens this side, is also by Simon, but it is not one of his better songs. It is somewhat predictable in structure, and the long repetitions of 'he' in the title eventually tire the ear, especially as there is hardly any harmonic interest to compensate. Death is close by, as the 'freedom rider' (to be transformed in 1969 into *Easy Rider*, a seminal film of the youth movement of the late 1960s) dies, but the date (June 1963) declares the 'brother' to be black, of the civil rights movement, which at that time was perhaps the most politically sensitive topic in the USA. In spite of the theme the song is not morbid, being expressed within a fast and attractive tempo, but this seems to work against it; meditations upon death, even violent death, demand a slower tempo for their fullest impact.

'Peggy-O', which follows, is a traditional folk song, beautifully sung with some superb harmonic touches and a delightful atmosphere, the whole thing acting as a light relief from the sombre mood of much of the material. But just as one has been lulled into this (false) sense of knowing what it is all about, this joyous atmosphere suddenly talks of destruction and death in an insidious manner. This fourth verse is almost like a con trick; we only realize what has happened after the event, and the innocence of the opening verses is here transformed into an anti-war song as the returning soldier himself seeks revenge. The only unanswered question is why does he seek revenge? A dozen answers suggest themselves, any one of which could fit, such is the expressive nature of this magnificent performance. 'Go Tell It On The Mountain' is an unnecessary addition to the album. It adds nothing to our knowledge of the duo, repeats many of the earlier sentiment that had been built up with such impressive consistency, and the performance is the weakest so far. It sounds a shade too fast for comfort, being faintly rushed and actually accelerating (unintentionally, no doubt) as the song progresses. Garfunkel himself sounds less than his suave self, and although the enthusiasm is notable the record would have been improved by the omission of this track.

At first 'The Sun Is Burning' appears as another anti-war song, an anti-nuclear one this time, but it fits the overall scheme of the album perfectly. It must be said at once that it receives a magnificent performance and

33

brings in a burst of bright, verdant springtime, but eventually night comes as the song progresses, and the sun comes to earth not as a life-enhancing force but as a destroyer. In later years Garfunkel might have said there was too much echo on his channel; it does not quite spoil the performance, but it almost does.

With such splendid and original songs as 'Bleecker Street', 'Sparrow' and 'The Sounds Of Silence' on the album it might at first seem odd to include Dylan's 'The Times They Are A-Changin'', but in fact it works perfectly. Any lingering doubts about the real nature of the album are now dispelled; the title of this song could well be the title of the album (were it not for the fact that confusion would reign). The theme of change, be it religious re-evaluation or musical re-evaluation (in 'Benedictus'), social unrest or even the times of day and the cycle of human life, is the true 'message' (if message is needed) of the album.

To those familiar with Dylan's performance, this one by Simon and Garfunkel is clearer but no less urgent and compelling. Because of its clarity the message of sympathetic, organic protest is thrown out towards the audience, and the listener is invited to participate in the movement. At the time this was recorded – 1964 – it can reasonably be supposed that the majority of the likely listeners of the day would have been aware of Dylan's masterpiece and the implications of parent–offspring relationships. And then, just when the listener feels he has Simon and Garfunkel identified, Simon holds the melody line and Garfunkel's voice is astonishingly much stronger than on any other song on the album. The effect is disconcerting; just the right sort of effect for this particular song.

'Wednesday Morning, 3 a.m.', the title of the album, now concludes it. We return to several things; the composer is Simon and the questions asked are not all answered. The intimacy, the personal imagery which was such a feature of Simon's songs on side one, is here revealed again, as the 'observer' is also the 'doer'. The religious features are very faint now, almost non-existent apart from the reference to 'pieces of silver', and the insidious feeling of guilt, of seeking forgiveness and absolution, is never entirely absent. This song is not quite in the same class as the others but it fulfils its purpose admirably; for the guilt of leaving, the admission of theft, and the faint quickening of tempo in the last few bars all combine to tell us that other journeys are to be undertaken, that the voyage is not yet over.

Thus does this remarkable first album end, and it is difficult not to be impressed by it. It is not without its faults, as we have seen, but its positive virtues are so strong that within several years its finest song, 'The Sounds Of Silence', had virtually become the Simon and Garfunkel signature tune, a theme that runs like a *cantus firmus* through their work, and that would, if nothing else had been written, have singled them out as masters of their art.

The main drawback to the album is its structure; the best song comes at the wrong moment and should have ended the album, not closed side one. If 'Wednesday Morning, 3 a.m.' had changed places with 'The Sounds Of Silence', the album would have finished in the best possible manner (always assuming that 'Go Tell It On The Mountain' would have been omitted) and such a change would have made more sense, especially the theme of forgiveness on 'Wednesday Morning, 3 a.m.' coming immediately after 'Benedictus'. One final point concerns the sleeve notes. Garfunkel's have already been mentioned, but there are additional notes by Ralph J. Gleason that do a certain amount of damage. They are

35

presumptuous and hyperbolic, and no self-respecting literate artists should have permitted their inclusion on the album.

1966

SOUNDS OF SILENCE
For track listings see Discography p. 148

It is important to bear in mind the point made in the previous chapter that this was the first Simon and Garfunkel album to be released in Great Britain. By this time, however, Paul Simon's first solo album, *The Paul Simon Songbook*, had also been released, and fascinating as that album is, it is surely one of the last full-length albums to have been issued by a major rock star who is the only performer on the record without overdubbing – Simon sings to his own guitar accompaniment. There is no double- or multi-tracking, and the nature of such a production almost invariably leads to the material being pigeon-holed into one area or another, whether the music justifies it or not. In Simon's case it was 'folk', and it may well have been the danger of neglecting such fine material as is contained on the solo album that led him to allow adaptation of several songs for the next Simon and Garfunkel release. The result is, however, somewhat disappointing, for in the course of this fresh instrumentation scant attention appears to have been paid to the essential nature of the material involved, with the result that several of Simon's most perfectly formed songs have been treated with as much sympathetic understanding as a poster-paint artist would have in adding to a watercolour miniature. A direct result was several hit versions by other singers, so the experiment could hardly be counted an unmitigated failure, and in any event only a handful of songs are thus spoiled, and all exist in alternative recordings of finer artistic quality.

The masterpiece of the first album, 'The Sounds Of Silence', opens this follow-up, at least on the British version, which would seem an unusual thing to do. But this is a 'bigger' sound, broader and frankly stodgier in appearance. The dull, enervating effect is due to the unsubtle addition of an unnecessary, raucous bass line, a florid and confusing (because it is in the same octave as Garfunkel's voice) electric guitar line and a squashed sound image that makes it virtually impossible to separate the voices. In one respect this does mean that the voices are blended, but the text of the song demands the light and shade, the distinctive tone colours of both Simon and Garfunkel. A result of this is that the words are largely incoherent, which may be a mixed blessing; this was the third successive album by Simon and Garfunkel (either singly or together) to include this song, and the feeling of familiarity is hard to overcome. As if this was not bad enough, the ensemble in the last chord is very poor and to sympathetic ears the result is bitterly disappointing.

'Leaves That Are Green' also comes from *The Paul Simon Songbook* and immediately goes a long way to righting the unsatisfactory opening track. The song is concerned with change, life-cycles and the nature of impermanence. It is a splendid song, intensely musical, with a superb change of key, sidestepping to the flat seventh (in this case C major within a D major tonality) which has the faintly giddying effect of being on a fairground ride only to discover that it lurches at off moments; not so much as to cause unease, but just enough to cause eyebrows raised. This happens at the words 'that are' every time the title comes round, but more surprises are at hand. The ending of the song is in the

37

wrong key – A major instead of D – and yet it is done with such style and assurance that momentarily we are fooled into thinking it the right key after all, mirroring the 'change' and impermanence of the subject. The arrangements are splendid, and include a highly appropriate harpsichord part that gives a gritty harmonic bite to the rhythm.

Harmonic irregularities, always finely controlled and allied to a properly expressive purpose, are to be found on the next song, a new one in context, 'Blessed'. On the surface it is one of those comparatively familiar anti-religious songs that young protesters have been compelled to pen from time to time, but it is not so much anti-religious as anti-hypocrisy. By parodying the Sermon on the Mount – one of the centrepieces of Christian belief – Simon possibly states his point with too great an emphasis; but it must be said that it is coupled with music wholly suitable to such treatment. It begins in an aggressive, Dylanesque manner, with loud driving minor chords in a broad 3/4 beat like a gallumphing, insensitive monster. Tearing across this fabric, almost literally so with the *major* mediant immediately countering the minor mediant of the introduction, the voice blares out the parodies as if flinging them back towards an audience for shock effect. The singer – such is the quality of Simon's writing that even at this reasonably early stage in his career one is forced to think of the singer as the personification of the writer, as well as being the object of the song – continues his parodies, but with such repetitious insistence and insensitivity that he in fact becomes the very thing he condemns: dogmatic and unthinking. The use of electric organ in the middle section has clear religious overtones, but the chording is very unusual, irregular and difficult to follow. The effect is exactly as one imagines the composer meant it to be –

disturbing, if not exactly provocative. As an example of its time this unusual outburst is a fascinating document, though as a piece of music it does not wear well. One suspects that the destructive, almost self-destructive, forces mostly at work in early Punk have a greater validity, although the time-scale is not yet comparable. But in one respect this song looks forward to the high-energy, raucous dirtiness of Punk — the coda contains a sudden, alarming change of sound image where a crude technical tape edit is all too apparent.

In complete contrast to this outburst 'Kathy's Song', which follows, is an intimate portrait, quietly delineating the lines with the fine shading of a pencil drawing. Garfunkel is absent on this track, the only voice being that of the composer, and the only instrumental timbre readily discernible that of acoustic guitar. There could hardly be a greater contrast with the previous 'Blessed', and we are immediately in the mould of *The Paul Simon Songbook* album. The song is of six verses and very simply constructed in two parts, each containing three verses, separated by a bigger guitar break between verses three and four. The words are obviously significant, and we might also discover that the lady in question meant a great deal to the singer at the time, but such is the smiling intimacy of the song that it goes against the grain to attempt any analysis. One feels that by so doing one is intruding on a very personal communion, and then one realizes the significance of the juxtaposition of 'Blessed' and 'Kathy's Song' on the album — there is no doubt which is the more genuinely sincere expression, perhaps the more blessed, the more stunning realization that God is Love. If this seems too fanciful it certainly fits the situation, both in words and music, and is a more than likely explanation. The touching simplicity of this song is best conveyed by the lengthy and deeply expressive solo

39

guitar coda. This could almost become a solo guitar piece if someone had the inclination to make it so, for it flowers and blossoms into the most beautifully played meditation on the musical gems which run through the song. It remains one of the best examples on disc of Simon's considerable artistry on the instrument.

'Somewhere They Can't Find Me' is another Paul Simon original, and on this track Garfunkel rejoins his partner. Like 'Kathy's Song' this is a good number, one of a handful of excellent songs by Simon at this time that – however well crafted and well presented they may be – just fail to ignite. It is a first-class album track but not especially memorable. Garfunkel's voice is not the only difference in timbre between this song and its predecessor, for a much fuller instrumentation is used, a full complement of woodwind, brass and strings all conspiring to hide the singing line, or if not to hide it then to make it more difficult to discern. In other words it is yet another profoundly musical expression of the title.

Having given us a brief demonstation of his guitar-playing prowess in the coda of 'Kathy's Song', Simon now moves again to the centre stage, discarding Garfunkel and the orchestra. The final track on this side is a guitar solo by 'Davy Graham, one of England's finest jazz/blues guitarists', as it says on the liner notes. During the sixties, and not a little helped by this very performance, Graham's quite attractive if not very individual instrumental became a virtuoso piece for an armada of aspiring (and already established) guitarists. Apparently Graham was in need of some kind of practical help at the time and Simon included this track to ensure the succeeding royalties would help the composer. Simon plays the piece well and it is a worthy example of his art, but it is a little disconcerting to hear such a track early on in the career of a duo of singers.

40

The result of this variety on side one is that the feeling of mixture is acute. The side is not well planned, for it was a mistake to end it with this instrumental, although by so doing it affords the nimble record collector the opportunity of lifting the stylus before this last track and keeping his listening experience concentrated on Simon and Garfunkel's singing performances.

Side two begins with 'Homeward Bound', at least for British record collectors (it is absent from the original American album). This is one of the duo's early successes in chart placings, and it is a very good song. Since Simon admitted that the song was written on Widnes railway station one night, waiting for the late train to London, the fact always has to be mentioned, but such is the composer's genuine sense of universality that northern England has inspired one of the best songs ever written about homesickness. And again, one has to qualify the description because however deeply moved the singer is by the vulnerability and loneliness of his position, it is done without that weeping anguish, the sentimental gimmickry that emotionally, often mawkishly, detracts from most other songs on the same subject. Knowing the circumstances surrounding the song's composition, one almost expects a quiet arrangement with just the two singers, Simon's guitar and perhaps an acoustic bass. What we get, however, is enough to send anyone home. The arrangement is unworthy of the material: a piano, a total irrelevance in context of music or lyric, obscures the fabric, and a zombie-like drummer, oblivious of the sensitive emotion the singers convey, punches out the crudest oneTWOthreeFOUR, cutting right across the natural shape of the song. This adds a further emotion, one of exasperation, which is alien to the spirit of the song. How this splendidly original number came to be accorded this kind of treatment is in artistic terms inexplicable. The record company, with hindsight, might claim that because this was a hit it does not matter, and anyway it worked, and because it was successful the success is its own justification. But anyone listening with half an ear to this track would have to have defective hearing not to appreciate that it might easily have been a greater success had the song been given a real chance, that of being itself.

'Richard Cory' is a marvellous song for Simon enthusiasts, offering much to argue over and to fascinate. It is an excellent song as music, being quite fluent, almost plastic in its total freedom, yet not so free as to induce that worst excess of the 1960s, 'free will'. The freedom comes as the composer refuses to force the song, as he so easily could have done, into a straitjacket, offering instead subtle changes of emphasis by adding two beats here or another two there, by delaying the establishment of the major tonality and by a variety of other devices all used to give the words the greatest impact and prominence. It is a remarkable composition, a superb achievement, and, unlike the previous song, is fully realized in sound terms to make the deepest impact on the sympathetic listener. It is difficult not to be sympathetic to the story of a man, outwardly successful and wealthy, with money, position and influence, and by all appearances at ease in his private life, who nevertheless is found one day to have deliberately shot himself, his secret dying with him. Of course, anyone can write a song on such a subject, but Simon's genius is such that he can point a moral without condescension, for we are forced at the end of the song to muse over the real values in life, in human relationships, and not to be bedazzled by the trappings of temporal power. If this sounds like preaching, it is not meant to be, for Simon can easily tread the fine dividing line between suggestion and insistence.

As if to make the point even more clearly – though one can again question the layout of this album because of it – the next song, 'A Most Peculiar Man', also concerns itself with a suicide. But it is the reverse of the Richard Cory episode. Cory was wealthy and in the public eye; here the man is unknown, quiet, anonymous and without friends or relations. Such a person we tend to say is one to 'keep himself to himself', but the result of such an inward-looking approach is to force the person deeper into the hidden recesses of his own mind – in which case suicide is the logical final step, there being nothing else to experience. The title comes from the man's neighbour, describing the tenant to an interested party, who could be a policeman, a newspaper reporter or a coroner. Apparently this too was inspired by a true event – reading of such a death in a London newspaper. But Simon has more to offer than mere description: he possesses great psychological insight. The fourth beat of the two-bar main phrase is accented by a kind of sonic snick, like a nervous twitch coming at regular intervals; could this be a facial characteristic of the disoriented dead man? True or not, in the last verse the tonal basis is 'attacked' by sudden irrational sounds, off the beat, as if the very fabric of emotional stability is about to collapse. It is as disturbing a feature as the song's story line.

Life reasserts itself in the next song, 'April Come She Will', already known from *The Paul Simon Songbook* album but here sung by Garfunkel. It is a touching, poised and classically restrained performance of a minor masterpiece, again juxtaposed for maximum impact, for the lyrics are a version of an old nursery rhyme. The contrast between children's innocence and the deaths of the two previous songs is underlined by such proximity. But with 'We've Got A Groovey Thing Goin'' we encounter an aspect of this composer that he has rarely explored. This is all to the good, for at best this is an effective parody of a certain type of popular song of the time. Perhaps it has to be seen in that light, because of the spelling of 'groovey' and the cryptic liner note of three words: 'just for fun'. It is disappointing, a massive irrelevance, with only the catchy beat having any redeeming feature.

The final number, 'I Am A Rock', another song from the *Songbook*, is treated with even less style and consideration than 'Homeward Bound', which is to say that it is ruined. A wild organist is let loose on the performance and does his best to spoil things. If one can stay to the end, the coda is worth hearing, if only once, but it beggars description.

And so ends an intermittently brilliant, occasionally infuriating, second album. What emerges above all is the intense creativity, which is not always controlled – when it is, it becomes irresistible. The mistakes are fewer, more musical and more forgivable, but the highspots are wholly memorable.

1966

PARSLEY, SAGE, ROSEMARY AND THYME
For track listings see Discography p. 148

This album, a distinct advance on *Sounds of Silence*, begins with an amazing and indestructible demonstration of genius. 'Scarborough Fair: Canticle', destined to become one of this duo's most classic creations, has caused some argument about whether the Scarborough Fair tune is original or not. It is claimed as such by the publishers, but it is an old folk song in origin. This matters little; what does matter, and what cannot be denied, is that the combination of the two songs into one is original and produces music that immediately burns into the mind to such an extent that it is impossible to listen to the folk song in an 'authentic' guise without feeling that something is distinctly lacking. In any event, the song's melody line on this album is an original version by Simon with sufficient changes to make it his own composition. The song begins magically with a timelessness, an other-worldly ethereal quality, with the effect of the duo singing in unison. One says effect, for it may be double-tracking, and it matters little either way. The instrumentation is fascinating – harpsichord, crotales, electric piano; a tintinnabulous cascade perceived from afar, which must have had a great effect (if not exactly influence) upon the young Mike Oldfield, who momentarily recalls this opening at the beginning of his masterpiece, 'Tubular Bells', and of Jim Webb (in the context a more significant influence) whose line 'how delicate the tracery' from his superb 'MacArthur Park' is brought to mind. At the words in 'Scarborough Fair', which start each second quatrain, 'Tell her to . . .', the second song begins, the Canticle, but placed aurally as an echo effect like some half-remembered parallel idea floating near the surface of the subconscious mind. There follows a gradual, hypnotic build-up of tension through the words of the Canticle (or rather those words of this song we are allowed to hear in the recording – following the published music is an aid to a fuller understanding, but the music must be heard as music, not as printed patterns). This collage – for such it is – keeps Canticle in the background, though we can perceive the last part of the lines, each one more urgent than its predecessor, all expressed within this dreamlike atmosphere. Consider how the tension mounts by the ends of these lines: 'deep forest green'; 'snow crested brown'; 'mountain' – all natural phenomena, untouched by man, followed by 'polishes a gun'; 'scarlet battalions'; 'to kill'; and finally 'long ago forgotten'.

The repeated phrase from which the album takes its title, 'parsley, sage, rosemary and thyme', moves always to the dominant of the key, and this affords a climactic key change just when it is needed. This, coupled with the urgent singing of 'Tell her . . .' and a constant 3/4 pulse, gives this slowly moving song its great sense of forward movement. The final statement of Scarborough Fair virtually abandons the accompanying instruments and the voices raise upwards towards the sky. The total effect is quite overwhelming.

'Patterns' drops a tone and bursts into life with new, more urban, musical imagery: the guitar is loud and pulls the key bluesward, bending the material, with a throbbing yet quietly insistent bass line on the left-hand channel against a constant pattern of repetitious three drums on the right. The voices and guitar (which is rarely used after they enter) are in the middle. These 'patterns' (i.e. the aural stereo layout) are always emphasized, yet the song concerns the words until the middle break for guitar. 'The rat dies'; suddenly the sound cuts the echo and tightens. The urban change of atmosphere is clear; 'street lamp' fixes the locale, but the acoustic guitar break by Simon refuses to be 'urbanized'. It is the personification of the 'observer', the singer of the song.

The next song, 'Cloudy', is a comparatively poor piece, the interest mainly centring on the imaginative arrangement. There is little melodic distinction and the words also seem to be more obscure than is usual with this writer. In terms of the planning of this album side, however, the song acts as an interlude, being undemanding and not possessing any facet that need concern us greatly.

'The Big Bright Green Pleasure Machine' is one of

Simon's few songs (perhaps the only one) that clearly demonstrates the influence of John Lennon. It is not difficult to imagine how the Beatles in their Magical Mystery Tour period would have done this. What the 'pleasure machine' is – the use of the word 'machine' dates the song somewhat – remains unknown. Spencer Leigh has suggested it might be a vibrator, and he may well be right; the lyrics (when they can be heard through the heavy-handed treatment) point this way, although 'green' is obviously chosen to rhyme with 'machine'.

Paul Simon whispers 'two . . . three . . .' and 'The 59th Street Bridge Song (Feelin' Groovy)' flickers into life. Superficially this has all the maturity of a cream puff, yet it remains a great achievement. First, the emotional tenor is light and airy, full of those half-grasped Hopkins-like coined words and phrases which in their very newness both attract and reassure us. Second, it is a very short song indeed (including Simon's spoken 'two . . . three . . .' it lasts a mere ninety-nine seconds), scherzando in effect, almost over before its time, but retaining all the fascination of a closely worked and perfectly finished miniature. The skill and imaginative detail fashioned on this buoyant and happy gem is proof of the artistic care of both Simon and Garfunkel. Such an approach would have been unthinkable on their first album.

And so we turn the disc over in a pleasant, relaxed frame of mind. We are reassured when 'The Dangling Conversation' begins, for the opening guitar notes of both this new song and the '59th Street' number are the same. There the resemblance ends, for 'The Dangling Conversation' is an incomparably deeper and more profound song. It is one of the finest songs ever written by a 'popular' musician. One puts 'popular' in inverted commas because on this showing Simon achieves an artistic statement of considerable quality.

The lyric has a fashioned, hard-worked strength and can (and should) stand by itself as a fine contemporary poem. Its literary allusions have nothing to do with this; the references to Emily Dickinson and Robert Frost are entirely appropriate to the central theme of the song, which, taken at face value, is of a couple unable to communicate at a deep personal level, whose topics of conversation are the trappings of their comfortable lives. The heartstopping thought, which possibly inspired the song, is that the man acknowledges the hopelessness of the situation and wants to return to happier times, but cannot bring himself to say so.

The music is equally impressive, being completely organic. The introduction approaches the key of the song by a circuitous route, and the bass line, as it rises and falls like the measured slow breathing of a reader, functions as a theme in itself. The 'couplets out of rhyme' (i.e. the grown apart couple of the song) is depicted musically by the fact that the melody hovers all around the main key without actually settling on it. This tonal fluidity produces some astonishing harmonic progressions, particularly the major flat seventh chord (a Simon fingerprint) first heard at 'couched in our indifference', then followed by the *major* a semitone below and the chord a tone below that. One does not have to be a musician to appreciate this. Play the record and listen at that point to the harmonies below and then listen for those same progressions in other contexts. This last chord is the dominant of the home key, but the return home is tantalizingly delayed, like something forever just out of reach. And this harmonic fall (a descending minor third) is precisely that which began the song, demonstrating the total musical control and artistic integrity of this masterly composition. The gradual introduction of a large string orchestra and harp is a further notable touch; the cello line (recalling the timbre in 'Benedictus') is beautifully played, surrounded by a soaring tutti violin line, the two joining to form a rich tapestry. Note also a final touch of genius – two quiet bass drum thumps in the coda, after 'matter' and 'said', perfectly placed to draw attention to the despair of the words and the human situation they convey.

'Flowers Never Bend With The Rainfall' is not on such an exalted level, but it displays some intriguing features. The imagery of the title is mirrored by the first twenty notes of the song, which are the same note repeated twenty times (i.e. never 'bending'), but it hardly merits as much attention as the masterpieces that surround it on this album.

No matter what is read into the title (which does not appear in the song), 'A Simple Desultory Philippic (Or How I Was Robert McNamara'd Into Submission)' is sensational. The impact and vivid imagery of this song are still capable, decades after it first appeared, of creating the most intense enthusiasm in the listener. One astonishing fact is that the vast variety of figures chosen as contemporary creators of a certain media type in the song mean as much today as they did in 1966, proof of Simon's acute artistic judgement. Not that such mentions make the song great in itself, for that is achieved by other means; the hard, dirty driving rhythm (surprising for such a composer), the solid delivery and the sexually suggestive semitonally rising and throbbing bass line, form the rock-hard (in every sense) foundations. Another is the feel the song has for the music of the time. It is either a song influenced by, or an affectionate parody of (one suspects the latter) Bob Dylan, who is obliquely referred to several times (and once directly) in the song. The reference to Dylan has been described as a jibe, but it surely is not. It concerns a man who had not heard of Bob

Dylan, only Dylan Thomas, and because of that the singer feels the man lacks culture. Far from being a jibe, this is a flattering reference. The references to drugs, to Garfunkel and to 'Albert' (when Simon drops his harmonica towards the end of the song) are light relief, but perhaps the most important of all these ingredients is the song's forward-looking aspect. Who could deny the strength of the influence this song, and others like it, has had on later stars such as David Bowie? The bass line is also reminiscent of The Who's 'My Generation', though it may be too much to claim an influence here. In this regard, the song is an amazing musical document.

In spite of the literary allusions some commentators have found in the title 'For Emily, Whenever I May Find Her' (the Emily allegedly being the American poet, Emily Dickinson), this is a simple song with regard to its musical content. Nor is 'simple' a euphemism for 'weak', yet it cannot be denied that this is not one of Simon's finest tunes. The lyrics are easily the best part of the song and deserve close study by themselves, but there is one unusual aspect of the song which has never been remarked upon. It is that the coda, at the very end, spreads out in a long, falling phrase to the words 'Oh, how I love you'. In both words and music this is echoed virtually note for note in the later Moody Blues track, 'Knights In White Satin'. This influence (it is almost too much for coincidence) would not be important in itself were it not for the fact that this track was issued on a single as the B side of a new song, 'A Hazy Shade of Winter' (not released in album form until eighteen months later). It is difficult, in view of the Procol Harum's later worldwide hit with 'A Whiter Shade Of Pale', not to suspect Simon's influence at work here.

'A Poem On The Underground Wall' is a wonderfully observed metropolitan cameo. The late night

Underground traveller (and it is the London Underground) sees a furtive man write a four-letter word 'deep upon the advertising'. Graffiti was less common in the mid-1960s than it subsequently became, but the poet's observance of the act is redolent of sexual imagery, not in the man's blatant manner or the word he wrote but in subtle pictorial touches. The Underground train, too, is musically caught by a throbbing bass drum (at first like the passing of time on a big old Underground station clock). The 'contemporary' feeling is conveyed in the title; the four-letter word is perceived as a *poem*.

The album comes to an end with another collage, but of a very different kind. Against a beautifully sung version of the old carol 'Silent Night', a broadcaster reads the seven o'clock news on the radio. It is a gloomy bulletin, full of war, death and human misery, but the emotional impact fails. The impression conveyed is that it is the intention of the duo to make the listener think about organized religion and the horrors of everyday organized life. It is embarrassingly unsubtle, like someone sticking one or two fingers up against an Oxfam poster, and induces the same 'So what?' reaction it clearly intends to portray. Had Paul Simon set the news bulletin to the tune of 'Silent Night' the point would have been much better made, because it would have been musically made.

3   Simon and Garfunkel recordings 1968 to 1982

1968

BOOKENDS
For track listings see Discography p. 149

The album begins with a simple guitar solo in triple time of somewhat forgettable cut entitled the 'Bookends Theme', which we later learn is a version of the song 'Bookends' (the published title, although the sleeve and label refer to the track as 'Bookends Theme'). After thirty seconds of this reverie we are immediately plunged into the urban drama of 'Save The Life Of My Child'. In many ways this is totally unlike anything they had done before, but in another it is the musical realization of the juxtaposition of 'Silent Night' and the 'Seven O'Clock News' of the previous album. It is a kind of musical collage with bits of action cleverly and fascinatingly blended into an almost operatic setting of the drama of a child (eventually we discover the child is almost adult) threatening to throw himself from a building. We hear the crowd, the anguished cries of the mother, the police, and, forcing its way through the menagerie, the opening bars of 'The Sounds Of Silence'.

It is a startling contrast to those previous Simon productions. In discussing the *Parsley, Sage, Rosemary and Thyme* album we noted one or two instances where Simon could have influenced later groups, but this track shows the (assimilated) influence of other pioneering albums of the late 1960s (perhaps the seminal influence being The Beatles' *Sergeant Pepper's Lonely Hearts Club Band*). The use of bits of material in the manner of a patchwork is cleverly blended so that it becomes a further development within a purely Simon and Garfunkel context. Some Simon experts, particularly Spencer Leigh, rate this song highly, but once one has removed the immense production effects, the song is comparatively unremarkable, even ordinary. This is best demonstrated by playing the song from the published music (which is at best an approximation of what we hear, the entire gamut of the collage being almost impossible to notate on paper). Is one convinced by the use of the flat seventh as a passing tonic (in this case F major within a G major tonality)? This would appear to be the only unusual thing about the song, and it is by no means rare in Simon's output. As mentioned earlier, music should be experienced as sound in time, not in any other way, be it a Beethoven symphony, a Wagner opera or a Bartok string quartet. On that level, 'Save The Life of My Child' remains a somewhat startling experience.

It leads immediately into one of Simon's greatest songs, 'America'. This is the most haunting and profoundly moving statement on his own country by a musical genius who had been so deeply influenced by the British rock scene of the mid-1960s and by his early interest in European folk song. Yet 'America' achieves more by innuendo and suggestion than by mere geographical description.

Consider the unusual bar grouping: basically a four-bar phrase, the song achieves an unusual subtlety by its faint changes of bar sequences. Another, more remarkable feature is the vivid images invoked by the simplest musical means and the distilled poetry of the lyric. We are passengers, observing the couple on the Greyhound bus, who in turn converse and talk about the other passengers as the vehicle speeds along the turnpike. The conversation ceases and we all quietly observe our surroundings, thinking of other things. 'Toss me a cigarette,' says the composer (Paul Simon), and sings solo. The girl (Kathy) replies with both voices, Garfunkel's being like a faint immediate echo; not a feminine voice, but a different one. Such tiny touches of creativity (and there are many) are masterly. Rarely enough, in view of some earlier songs, the lovers here communicate easily; it is a totally relaxed atmosphere, intimate, with gentle strokes and brief gestures, half smiles. The girl sleeps with her head resting on her lover's shoulder. He is awake, thinking perhaps of the Mrs Wagner pies they brought for the journey. The whole thing is quite overwhelming in its impact and deeply felt emotion, yet all expressed with a fine simplicity and beauty.

The cigarette is lit between songs (one hears it so, and the first draw being inhaled as it travels across the channels) and, in utter contrast once more, we hear the opening music of 'Overs'. This is a resigned, faintly bitter piece on the end of a relationship. Like 'America', much is achieved by a sparse use of imagery; polite encounters, but the fire has gone out. The song is not the kind of thing one wants to hear often, but the *double entendre* of the final line, 'I stop and think it over', is a fine touch.

The decaying embers of the relationship are startlingly taken up in the next track, 'Voices Of Old People'. This is a true collage of scraps of monologue and conversation of elderly people, often with one word acting as the link between one voice and the next. The result is an effective and sometimes moving corrective to any anodyne feelings which might remain; in context, it works admirably. Like the previous track this is not one to play often, but there is always something deeply touching and childlike, and therefore innocent and vulnerable, about elderly people reminiscing at will.

Although non-musical this track leads naturally to the final song, 'Old Friends', and appropriately so, for 'old' here means both elderly and/or long-standing. The Beatles' *Sergeant Pepper* contained a song about getting old – 'When I'm 64' – but that was not a serious piece; in Simon's song the singer has a vision of himself and his partner when they themselves are old, and he imagines what must go through the minds of elderly people today. This is yet another major achievement for Simon. Like 'Saturn, the Bringer of Old Age' in Holst's *The Planets*, the slowness and unremitting passing of time is conveyed by a slow tempo with long note values, the soft, squashy harmonies, the deliberate 3/4 tempo, relieved by its first cousin, 6/8, gently rocking to and fro like inexpressible memories of long ago. It is strange for a young man to imagine himself being seventy but, as the singer realizes, the chances are he will be.

The friends sit 'like bookends' on the park bench, giving the album its title. The sensitivity and understanding of Simon's lyrics are wholly remarkable, and it was courageous too, for a young man in such a situation to address himself to the problems of the elderly. But the song does not end with words; during it various orchestral instruments have entered until at its close a whole orchestra is playing. Now, perhaps owing a little to 'A Day In The Life' from *Sergeant Pepper*, the orchestra expands into an atonal fantasy worthy of Boulez or Maxwell Davies in its disintegration of organic matter. It is a temporary thing; the original key returns to acknowledge the continuity of life. The 'Bookends

Theme' returns now under a high violin line, full of memory and experience. How far we have travelled from the first hearing of this tune, less than fifteen minutes ago.

If this side does not quite possess the complete organic unity which some commentators have noted, it is still a remarkable achievement. The second side is a collection of apparently unconnected songs and begins with 'Fakin' It'. This song offers a field day for the searchers after truth, but the message is hard to grasp. One concludes that it can mean almost anything one wants it to mean, but to the present writer it seems to be a completely sexual expression, albeit from a hazy, faintly drugged viewpoint. It begins with a fine, easy rhythm that accelerates in each bar, constantly surging and providing an eruptive sexual undertone. The song shows a curious connection with Lennon and McCartney songs, a touch of 'Paperback Writer' and 'Lady Madonna' perhaps, though the sentiment of the Simon song is more serious than either of The Beatles' tracks. There is surely a further connection with 'Old Friends' from side one, giving the lie to the commonly held belief that the first side is complete within itself. The falling triplets in this song reinforce the 'fakin' it' line, which might just be a euphemism for a much more direct and straightforward sexual utterance. The tonal scheme is also noteworthy; the keys fall, first by a tone, then a half-tone, from the tonic, and this dragging sensation coupled with the rising, accelerating bass line produces a squashy and very powerful image of impacted hard-focusing. Curiously enough, the parlando middle section, in which our hero goes off at a tangent to reminisce over how things might have turned out for him had he taken up tailoring, is frequently misquoted. As Spencer Leigh says, 'A shop door opens and a girl, Beverley Martin, asks a Mr Leitch if he's been busy. We know that's Donovan's surname

57

and so we decide it's an oblique reference to him.' All this would be plausible enough, though it does seem to be stretching things somewhat, were it not for the fact that in the printed music the gentleman enquired after by the girl is spelled 'Mr Leach'. While it is true that the printed music occasionally differs from the sung versions, this is concerned only with one or two words, not the spellings. It is extremely unlikely that Simon, the fastidious wordsmith, would have made it even more difficult to understand the odd reference to Donovan if the gentleman's real name was incorrectly spelled. Maybe there is another Mr Leach in the pop music business. Of such comparative trivia are claims made and rebuffed, but all this would not matter very much if we did not know that Paul Simon's ability as a lyricist was of the highest order.

After the heftily produced 'Fakin' It' the solo acoustic guitar with its major seventh comes with the relief of slipping on a warm, favourite jacket to begin 'Punky's Dilemma'. The delayed entry of the bass is in marked contrast to the bass-heavy line of the previous song, but it works perfectly, as we leave England (in spite of a passing reference to muffins) for Los Angeles and southern California. Beach Boy harmonies are not a million miles away and there is surely a none too obscure reference to what the young protesters in song were doing to avoid the draft; indeed, by the last verse it has become the most important question. But this is not the only part of Punky's dilemma; there is a hallucinatory aspect to the music that suggests familiarity with the teachings (if not the prescriptions) of Dr Timothy Leary, and is again obliquely referred to in the coda, where whistling idly the opening bars of 'I Was High And Mighty'.

Such references, not too difficult to discern, are sometimes claimed for the next song, one of the most famous of all Simon and Garfunkel recordings, 'Mrs Robinson'. This is crystal clear in its expression but because of the occasional hidden meanings it would appear that some have tried to read more into it than they should. Assuming for a moment that a knowledge of the film *The Graduate* is not a prerequisite for a full appreciation of the song, the overriding aspect is the profound sympathy and understanding of the frailties of the human condition. If this seems hyperbolic, consider for a moment the words themselves. Clearly Mrs Robinson has sinned: 'We'd like to know a little bit about you for our files', and she is now institutionalized. The line 'put it in your pantry with your cupcakes' must surely imply hashish, rather than the pill. Mrs Robinson is behaving in a way more commonly associated with a younger generation. 'Ev'ry way you . . . lose': therefore this has been no answer, but why should she seek one anyway? The kind of hero to whom as a younger girl she would have looked for inspiration, in this case the baseball player Joe DiMaggio, has 'gone away', leaving her without heroes and with the eternal truth of religious consolation, which she will probably reject. The final, curt 'Hey, Hey, Hey' implies this, and therefore the reference to Jesus loving her is not sensationalism but a straightforward statement. The matter of fact manner in which this somewhat surprising alternative is presented has led many people to overlook the fact that it is there, and clearly so, and is repeated quite often, in a 'Lo, I am with you always' manner. The juxtaposition of adjacent major chords above a freewheeling scalic rhythm bass and the clearest and most perfect harmonies for the duo all combine to make this a classic recording of quite timeless qualities. One final point: the left-hand channel fades at the end to let the right-hand continue alone, as though the protagonists walk off to their next patient.

The next song, 'A Hazy Shade Of Winter', although it dates from before most of the rest of the album, is another remarkable achievement. The 'winter' is a dim realization of mortality, an echo of the elderly folk on side one. Time has gone by, the leaves are brown, hopes and possibilities have vanished in the past. But it is viewed from the present, as the driving youthful rhythm makes plain. This song will never become popular in a wide sense but there is a superb quality about it; immense rhythmic life, quite fearless in its perception of the impermanence of all manner of things. Surprisingly, this song does not fade (one of the few occasions when such a course would have been justifiable on almost all grounds), but it is immediately (less than a second later) followed by 'At The Zoo'. At first this is a puzzlingly irrelevant creation. The various musical elements succeed one another without much discernible purpose and the 'message', in so far as it can be ascertained at all, is an anti-human humanization of animal characteristics. As such it is a puzzlingly inconclusive end to a brilliant album. On one level the whole album, *pace* the commonly held belief, can be seen as an almost total conception of varying aspects of humanity until, with the final song, animal symbolizations take over. As it fades, rather too quickly for comfort, this outstanding album ends with a faint unanswered question.

1968

THE GRADUATE
(with additional music by David Grusin)
For track listings see Discography p. 149

This album was issued at the same time as *Bookends*, and is invariably treated as a Simon and Garfunkel album even though their contributions are minimal and the songs they sing are available on other albums. The first track, 'The Sounds Of Silence', is a disappointing use of the remixed poor version on the *Sounds Of Silence* album. The tracks 'Mrs Robinson' and 'Scarborough Fair – Canticle' listed on side one are nothing of the sort. They are brief instrumental versions of bits of the main melody line picked out in somewhat hesitant manner by a guitarist who one fervently hopes is not Paul Simon; the playing is rather poor and the recording even more so, with distracting fingerboard noises and a distant fragment of sleigh bells (or so it seems) as a weird echo in the far distance. Maybe something else was being recorded in an adjacent studio. 'April Come She Will' is taken from the *Sounds of Silence* album. Quickly turning the disc over, the reprise of 'Scarborough Fair – Canticle' sounds suspiciously like the identical performance on the *Parsley, Sage, Rosemary and Thyme* album redubbed twice and played thus in succession, separated by a badly recorded flute (or ocarina) solo. There is no discernible difference at all between both complete statements of the song, a remarkable achievement for all the musicians involved. 'The Big Bright Green Pleasure Machine' comes over as an edited and speeded-up version of the earlier performance, now overloaded with lurid music. The version of 'Mrs Robinson' is not fit to be compared with that on *Bookends*; it sounds like a rough run through, an early stab at the song. Whole phrases are different from the published version and the brief, loud chords sound most peculiar.

If this album has been summarily dismissed so far, it is because of the clearly obvious musical defects contained upon it; it is fine for those wanting a memento of a seminal and highly successful film, but for those curious to understand the Simon and Garfunkel phenomenon it does the duo few favours. The album is partly redeemed (but only partly) by the final track, which is a new and elsewhere unavailable performance of the complete 'Sounds Of Silence'. The duo's voices are accompanied by what could well be just one acoustic guitar, drums being absent throughout, and although they are not terribly well recorded, this album is therefore a must for the Simon and Garfunkel enthusiast. It is fascinating to hear the fifth verse hummed, not sung, in a dreamy, ethereal state, but it is the only version recorded by Simon and Garfunkel where, at the end, they both clearly sing 'sound of silence' and not the more usual 'sounds of silence' – a small point but worth noting, especially when confusion reigns supreme over the correct title of the song.

1970

BRIDGE OVER TROUBLED WATER
For track listings see Discography p. 149

This world-famous record, one of the classic albums in all post-war popular music, is the high-water mark for Simon and Garfunkel's career; it was also their swan song. It was quite clearly planned as such, and although the immense international success it generated doubtless posed enormous difficulties in dealing with CBS, who were quite naturally most anxious to get them to follow it up with another album as soon as practicable, it is a measure of both artists' strength of character that they stuck to their guns. The opening song, 'Bridge Over Troubled Water' is arguably their most famous creation; it is also one of Paul Simon's simplest songs. Considering the time (1970) when it appeared, it was a startlingly risky business to begin the album with a lengthy ballad,

62

for a long time accompanied by nothing more than a piano. This has nothing at all to do with rock 'n' roll, but it succeeds admirably and in so doing adds several cubits to the range and expressive power of this remarkable pair of musicians. The opening piano chords, spaciously and solidly played by Larry Knechtel in the most stately manner, are quite arresting, but the whole conception is made by Garfunkel's magnificent interpretation of the hauntingly simple melody line. There are three verses, the first just with Garfunkel and the piano, yet the entire song has the feel of a single complete take, so inexorable and finely paced is the sense of growing power and strength. Garfunkel is incomparable; listen to the second time he sings the word 'a' in the title. He incorporates, entirely spontaneously it seems, a tiny curl of four short notes, decorating the line, almost playing with it but not in a flippant manner; rather that of a person supremely confident of his ability and able to change things at will without losing sight of the main objective. Such tiny touches as these add so much to the overall build-up, and any self-respecting singer would do well to study this performance, preferably with the music before him as well. In verse two the tiniest suggestion of vibraphone tone acts as a halo around the solo voice and the gradual build-up, finely controlled over the longest possible time span, is enormously impressive. The piano here deliberately 'crushes' the note, almost in a country style, perhaps most familiar from the slow playing of Floyd Cramer, but all this is done very rarely, with the greatest discretion, and it is over before one really has a chance to realize what has occurred. The tension is gradually stretched until, in the longish instrumental break before 'verse three' (not so designated, and beginning with different music, but formally fulfilling the function of a third verse), three bars before the voice re-enters, the electric bass guitar enters for the first time, a magnificent moment, the effect all the more remarkable for being so long delayed. Now Simon himself joins his colleague, and other instruments also enter the scene, notable being a large string section, the violins soaring with vibrant passion. This re-entry of the voice is to the words 'Sail on silvergirl, sail on by', a phrase which set many a commentator looking for hidden meanings. A clean hypodermic needle for injecting heroin was one fanciful claim, and the onset of premature greyness by Paul Simon's recently married young wife was another, but in 1972 Simon himself explained in the introduction to the collection *The Songs of Paul Simon* published by Michael Joseph: 'I got the idea for the lyrics while listening to a Swan Silvertones' recording of "O Mary Don't You Weep". The "sail on silvergirl" was written in the studio several weeks after I had completed the first two verses . . .' The song builds inexorably to its grandiose conclusion, made all the more thrilling by the high full major chord on the divided violins held, it seems, for an eternity long after the other instruments have stopped.

After such an opening it must have been almost impossible to find a suitable follow-up, but 'El Condor Pasa (If I Could)' could not be improved upon. It is, rightly, a complete contrast. The instrumental timbre is utterly new on a Simon and Garfunkel record, for it is a recording for the Philips Records company by the ethnic instrument band Los Incas and is itself an arrangement of an eighteenth-century Peruvian folk melody by Jorge Milchberg. To this unlikely and already complete track Simon added words to form a haunting and classic new song in its own right. Furthermore, he sings it, clearing the acoustic of Garfunkel's distinctive timbre, and the key is a semitone higher than 'Bridge Over Troubled

Water'. The effect is like consuming the lightest and most palatable lemon sorbet after a rich course, and the transformation is complete. It is equally hypnotic; nor could it by any stretch of the imagination be termed a gimmick, for the taste and skill lavished upon this remarkable recomposition are wholly admirable. Philips Records gave their full approval for their recording to be used and it is a measure of the skill of the CBS engineers that unless one had some idea of the studio work involved, one would never guess what had had to be done. Compared with the clear diatonality of the opening song, 'El Condor Pasa (If I Could)' curls semitonally around like a caterpillar.

After such strong drama and the unsophisticated directness of the Peruvian theme the mood is lightened by a humorous song of infectious vitality: 'Cecilia'. The words suggest that the young lady has been two-timing, but all is forgiven. She seems to be that kind of girl. The remarkable achievement here is that the beat is both solid and at the same time light, a result of using similar-sounding instruments to those just experienced on 'El Condor Pasa'. For all the happiness it does have an unreal quality, like a weird dream perceived through a kind of false smile.

A ferocious outburst, violent and heavy with apparently unnecessary brass writing, begins 'Keep The Customer Satisfied'. The use of trombones adds nothing to the song apart from a sense of self-indulgence. It is concerned with the rigours of being a touring musician, but the lightness of touch demands that the song should not be taken too seriously. This is a rare track for the duo, rocking along with the best of them and seeming to enjoy every minute of it. The strangely titled 'So Long, Frank Lloyd Wright' is considered in detail in chapter 6, not because it has qualities far above those of other songs here but because it has been chosen as an archetypal song with some unusual features, a detailed examination of which would do much to demonstrate Simon's unique qualities. One could just as easily have chosen the next number, 'The Boxer', a wonderful song on every level. As Simon revealed in an interview with Richard Green in the *New Musical Express* in 1969, '. . . it was recorded all over the place, the basic tracks in Nashville, the end voices in St Paul's Church, the strings in New York Columbia Studios and the voices there too. And the horns in the church.' A dozen years or so later, in the middle of a world recession and with unemployment in the Western world at an all-time high, such profligate spending of a company's resources seems utterly unjustified, and is a classic example of how artists let success go to their heads and demand all sorts of things that any self-respecting record company ought to resist. After all, would the record have sold any fewer copies had the fine Nashville studios been used for the strings, and if necessary, which seems highly unlikely, the voices and horns recorded in one of that city's excellent churches, rather than in New York? What difference could it conceivably have made? However, Clive Davis (then CBS's president) would have claimed that the record was one of the biggest selling in the history of the record business, and so the end result amply justified the means. Be that as it may, let us concern ourselves with the finished product.

This song is of the highest quality; it begins quite simply with a rather bald statement of the first six lines. Then the harmonies begin, sweet thirds, significant in themselves for the song oscillates between the major and the relative minor (in other words, a third below). It shifts gently into the minor at the refrain 'Lie la Lie', and is accompanied by the merest hint of a quicker tempo, but before then we have an irregular and other-worldly image, a nineteen-bar instrumental solo line, ringing with overhanging church acoustic. The locale is New York, the fighter not necessarily a pugilist but someone determined to make his way against the odds in the world. The whores on Seventh Avenue fix Manhattan, but only after two lengthy verses have left the question unanswered. There is a massive coda, the personification of strength, and then suddenly the orchestra has gone, leaving the sole guitar of the observers' accompaniment to recall the patterns from which this wholly unusual song has grown.

'Baby Driver', although on the face of it a pleasant enough number, is ultimately disappointing. Curiously the ingredients are quite brilliant; the music has considerable verve and the collage effects never impinge on the song or the listener's ability to hear the lyric. What is arguable, however, is the meaning behind the lyric, and the missing element Spencer Leigh complains of in *Paul Simon: Now and Then*, p.57: 'something is missing' is the quality that makes us wish to return again to the song, to dig beneath the surface lyric to find the real meaning of the words. On the face of it the words are insignificant. It is only because we know this artist is capable of so much that we feel let down when he is less than at his peak. Some claim a sexual innuendo to the phrase 'I wonder how your engine feels' but this seems wrong, until one listens to the words. The sleeve is wrong, three times. Simon and Garfunkel actually sing 'I wonder how your engines feel', which is quite another matter and could mean nothing more than labial pleasures.

From time to time we have noted how Simon likes to place songs in pairs, next to each other, as contrasting aspects of a similar idea or moods. As time goes by this becomes a notable fingerprint, and here after 'Baby Driver' is another New York song, 'The Only Living Boy

67

In New York'. Although a few clues are given the code is not hard to crack. At the time this album was being put together both Simon and Garfunkel were under great pressure to visit Hollywood to write the music for another film after the phenomenal success of the music for *The Graduate*. Simon refused, but Garfunkel, doubtless prompted by their joint decision to split up for a while after the *Bridge* album had been finished, accepted a part in Mike Nicholls' next film, *Catch 22*. So when Simon writes 'Tom . . . I'll know your part will go fine, Fly down to Mexico,' (where the film was to be shot), it is clearly Garfunkel who is being addressed. 'Tom', of course, was Garfunkel's pseudonym when they were Tom and Jerry, and Simon sings this song alone. The connection is complete and the song is revealed as an affectionate tribute from Paul Simon to his partner, who goes off on his new career with his blessing.

Having journeyed, the title of the succeeding song, 'Why Don't You Write Me?', would seem to be another 'connecting' song. Would seem to be, rather than is, for this lyric is obscure. The addressee is in the jungle anxious to hear news from his friend, and the previous Thursday drank half a bottle of iodine, though for what purpose is also not made plain. As Spencer Leigh says,' "Why Don't You Write Me?" is simply an extension of its predecessor while "Bye Bye Love" is surely deliberately placed after them as a comment on their break-up.' This is all very plausible, and Leigh offers the most sensible explanation for the running of these songs. The inclusion of 'Bye Bye Love' is surprising without such a reason, being an old hit of the Everly Brothers, the rock duo who had such an influence on the early development of Simon and Garfunkel. If they were planning to separate, then a version, which implies a reminiscence, of such a reminiscence (and their first recording of an Everly

68

Brothers number) would be highly appropriate. In which case, what is the last song, 'Song For The Asking', doing here? The answer is that it is nothing less than the album itself. The *Bridge Over Troubled Water* disc constitutes the 'song' 'for the asking' (i.e. any time the listener wants it he puts it on his record-playing equipment). 'This is my tune for the taking', 'ask me and I will play' – these are clear references to the disc itself, taking on the *persona* of the singer and inviting the listener to avail himself of the opportunity any time he feels like it.

This, then, is the most surprising conclusion to a most surprising album. Contained within the most successful recording CBS had issued for many years was a clear indication that it was to be the last. It is to be doubted whether anyone fully realized the implications of the lyrics.

1972

SIMON AND GARFUNKEL'S GREATEST HITS
For track listings see Discography p. 149

Two years after the phenomenally successful *Bridge Over Troubled Water* album, which had been in the British album charts for virtually the whole of that period, it was obvious that Simon and Garfunkel were in no mood to collaborate on another album, and indeed both had ideas for solo albums. And so the idea of the 'Greatest Hits' album was born. Anyone with half an interest in popular music knows what such an album is, but it is often the first sign that the artist has peaked in popularity, and often contributes to such a peak. It follows that a greatest hits album cannot include subsequent hits, and so these have to go on 'volume two'.

No volume two ever sold as well as volume one, for the simple reason that the average record buyer would rightly think that volume one contains all the best ones and volume two the less popular.

In Simon and Garfunkel's case, however, there were overriding reasons for a new album, at least as far as the market-place was concerned. There was no follow-up to *Bridge* in sight and, judging by the pace at which the duo worked, it would be a number of years at least before a 'volume two' could be contemplated. But the amazing fact about this album is that it was perfectly possible to compile a very strong album of genuine hits (all too often a 'greatest hits' compilation is fleshed out with tracks that stretch one's understanding about what makes a 'hit'), from a recorded repertoire of just five previous albums and to include a massive fourteen tracks – or in fact thirteen, for one is the *Bookends* instrumental theme. Nor is this all; we have learned how often several songs would appear in various guises on succeeding albums, so the actual variety of repertoire available to the compiler was even less than might at first appear. In terms of the ratio of hits to recorded songs, Simon and Garfunkel's must have been the highest in the world.

In an attempt (in the event, very successful) to add variety to the album, a number of alternative performances of the hit songs were included, and these live recordings make a very welcome change. It has been cleverly done, too; 'For Emily, Whenever I May Find Her' is a magnificent live recording, the engineers perfectly capturing the timbre and fine balance of the singers with a superb sense of space. The performers respond with a freer, more passionate guitar line than in the studio version and the whole is quite outstanding. 'The 59th Street Bridge Song' likewise is a live version, though it is not quite in the same class as the previous live track: it is good but not flawless. Some confusion has arisen concerning the next track, 'The Sounds Of Silence', which is faded in under the dying applause for the previous song. This gives the effect of a live recording, but it is the studio 'Sounds of Silence' version. The silent ending and the absence of audience noises prove that. 'I Am A Rock' sounds as though it has been remixed for the album, and the remaining live tracks, 'Homeward Bound' and 'Kathy's Song', reach a high standard. The other performances on this record have already been discussed, so they do not need further comment.

1981

THE SIMON AND GARFUNKEL COLLECTION
For track listings see Discography p. 150

This fine collection, by no means the *Greatest Hits* album under another name, was aggressively marketed in the United Kingdom as part of a television campaign. The result was hugely successful, but the album is listed here for completeness' sake only. The versions included are all studio recordings that had already been issued at least once before.

1981

THE CONCERT IN CENTRAL PARK
(Recorded live in Central Park, New York City, 19 September 1981)
For track listings see Discography p. 150

The circumstances surrounding this extravaganza have already been related earlier in this book. It is symptomatic that the previous CBS album, *The Simon and Garfunkel Collection*, found space for seventeen titles on two sides whereas this Geffen double album requires four sides for nineteen tracks. Nor is this due just to middle-age spread: sixty-eight minutes total playing time for four sides is poor value, especially when much more was recorded (including new material never before issued on disc) and could easily have been accommodated on the set.

The performances, as we shall see, are variable. In the circumstances this is perhaps only to be expected, but the recordings, too, take some time to settle down and get into their stride. When one considers the fastidious approach Simon is known to have adopted during his concert tours in the 1970s one might reasonably ask why proper sound balances were not carried out earlier, so the listener would not have to pay to hear people learn their craft. This is most noticeable on the opening track, a very disappointing, 'cold' version of 'Mrs Robinson'. The balance is poor, with a hint of distortion and little or no stereo separation. The inevitable crowd scenes would have been more suitable for 'Save The Life Of My Child'. 'Homeward Bound' also disappoints, but for different reasons. It is not 'tight' enough and is transformed into a medium bounce number. It is a long way from Widnes. The third track is yet another disappointment, for the performance itself is so sleepy and indolent. This is 'America', and the dewy-eyed freshness of the original 3/4 song is here changed into a heavy 12/8, sluggish and faintly uncaring.

With 'Me And Julio Down By the Schoolyard' things get better, and after that much better. This is the best performance so far and the recording is less offensive. The final track on side one is 'Scarborough Fair', which is extremely well sung and the recording is now much better balanced. The only thing to mar this track is the somewhat dragging tempo, which roots this performance of the classic song firmly to the spot.

'April Come She Will' is another very well sung performance by Garfunkel, but the fire is lacking; there is no excitement, no youthful sexual anticipation here, just a faintly blasé rendering. 'Wake Up Little Susie', the old Everly Brothers hit, presumably put in for old times' sake, is not the kind of thing that leads one to expect a re-creation of the Everly Brothers, but this version is too heavy-handed by far (principally because the recording is bass-heavy) for what is in essence a light and airy number. Simon's 'Still Crazy After All These Years' is an unfortunate piece of self-indulgence, not at all helped by a damaging organ part that all but smothers the singer. It certainly detracts from whatever enjoyment would have been there. The 'American Tune' is much better, and this more beefy sentiment seems to suit the occasion more. The final song on side two, taken from Paul Simon's Warner Brothers album *One-Trick Pony* and titled 'Late in the Evening', is the best so far. In fact, although the brass is somewhat bass-heavy the playing is electrifyingly good and the sound is not inappropriate to this song. Curiously enough, this performance comes over better than on the *One-Trick Pony* album, which has a somewhat antiseptic air about it. This really is very fine.

Side three begins with another (comparatively) recent Simon song, 'Slip Slidin' Away'. This is a fine extended version, well balanced and recorded with a genuine feel of growth. The tempo is ideal and the whole has that aura of relaxed and easy power which is very impressive. One can certainly sense that by now the performers have got fully into their stride. The next song, 'A New Heart in New York', is by Gallagher and Lyle, and oddly enough the descending five-note phrase which it has shortly after

73

the start is identical to that in 'American Tune' (or rather in this case, the Lutheran adapted tune). The performance is excellent and is superbly controlled. Two good songs now follow: the first is 'Kodachrome', which is very good, but then as it is such a good song it has to be. Chuck Berry's 'Mabellene' is terrific, a real rock 'n' roll performance, driving, urgent, insistent and irresistible. This is perhaps the most pleasurable performance on the set, which certainly cannot be said of the live rendering of 'Bridge Over Troubled Water' that follows. The piano is poor; it is out of tune and the sound poses severe problems for the recording engineer. Garfunkel seems a little nervous at first, being unable to relax and so put the song over as it demands. But these flaws are not great and conversely add a new element, that of growing tension. As a result the emotion builds inexorably to a splendid statement of the coda.

'Fifty Ways To Leave Your Lover' begins the final side and receives another good, dependable performance from Simon, with excellent backing from the band. The instrumental breaks are quite long and the song ends with superb solo drumming from Steve Gadd. There would seem to be one miscalculation; the atmosphere should have generated a reprise of one or other verses. 'The Boxer' is a severe disappointment. The duo sound uncommitted and tired, and the self-indulgence that has largely been held in check is here allowed full expression. Nor are the voices well blended, and they are occasionally out of tune. This is then followed by what seems to be the longest crowd applause of the evening, far too long for a record; after several minutes of this roar one has to check that there is still more to hear on the record. As if to compensate for this, 'Old Friends' receives a very good performance indeed. This must have made an indelible impression on the crowd, for the sense of atmosphere is strong. 'The 59th Street Bridge Song' is spoiled by crowd catcalls and other noises off. The ending is rather too much a tongue-in-cheek affair to be convincing.

After this a lone voice in the crowd calls out for 'The Sounds Of Silence' and after a short speech from Paul the classic song begins. This is not a great performance but it is a highly sentimental occasion, charged with emotion. As if to settle the matter once and for all, at the very end Garfunkel clearly sings 'sounds', yet the lines 'People bowed and prayed/To the neon god they made' could have seemed a little uncomfortable.

After all, half a million people were there that evening; to see the gods they had made? Whatever they came for, it is safe to assume they found it, and we can recapture those parts of the concert in Central Park whenever we wish. In many ways the resultant discs could have been better, but not by much in the technical sense. The trouble is that there are too many less than satisfactory performances to make it really memorable, and possibly the whole thing was overambitious. They had not played in public as a duo for many years and the tension and hesitancy took a long time to leave them. On balance it was probably right to have given the concert and to have recorded it, but the seeker after truth will find it better expressed on the earlier albums.

4 Paul Simon recordings 1965 to 1983

1965

THE PAUL SIMON SONGBOOK
For track listings see Discography p. 151

Such is the clarity and natural balance of the recording that every nuance, the slightest emphasis, is crystal clear. The words of the first song, 'I Am A Rock' are surprising: the singer appears proud of his ivory-tower existence, his cutting-off of most normal forms of human companionship and intercourse. 'I' cannot be him. He would have made a better point had he transferred to the third person singular, but it would have lost its immediacy. We would have remained less than totally convinced of Simon's commitment to the message. It cannot be Simon for another reason. The song is an anti-human message: no man is an island, and the net result of such an existence will become clear enough later on. But the imagery and literary qualities of the lyric are remarkable. The alliteration of 'freshly fallen silent shroud of snow' raises the lyric to a high plane of achievement. The illusions conjured up by the story, and the locale, declare this artist to be one of no mean ability. Quite apart from these deeper qualities, the song is magnificently performed. The third and fourth lines of the lyric are sung slightly ahead of the beat, in classic rock style, though the song is anything but rock music. The result is that the emotional tenor rises perceptibly at these moments, until it bursts into the arrogant claim 'I am a rock, I am an island'.

The wintry image continues in the next song, 'Leaves That Are Green'. It is the turning of the year. The leaves turn brown, wither and crumble. We learn the reason for the loneliness — the girl has gone, 'faded in the night'. 'Hello hello, goodbye goodbye' begins the last verse, with much repetition of 'goodbye'. When one thinks of the Lennon/McCartney song of 1966 'Hello/Goodbye' (not quite with the same theme, but very similar) there is no doubt that at this stage Simon was the deeper artist.

'A Church Is Burning' is another remarkable song of startling imagery and courage. It is an anti-Ku-Klux-Klan protest, but not at the essentially anti-Christian bigotry that such an organization displays. The strength of the song comes from the realization that a spiritual belief can never be destroyed. The tangible, physical appurtenances of such a belief may therefore wither and fade, or be smashed, but the soul is immortal. As Judith Piepe so well says in her liner notes: 'A church which fulfils her prophetic duty to preach justice, denounce the oppressor, demand freedom, will always be burning, with the fire of petrol and the fire of the human and Holy spirit.'

This is a very unusual subject for a 'popular' singer; and it is the only time that Simon recorded the song. Perhaps the singer of the first song has other qualities to sustain him in his loneliness.

To quote Michael Tippett's *A Child of Our Time*: 'The moving waters renew the earth. It is spring.' 'April Come She Will' is the start of the song; the '-il' sound in 'April' and 'ill' in 'will' are echoed in all the succeeding couplets

– 'May – stay' and so on through the summer months. We are reminded of the impermanence of all relationships – change, no matter over how long a time, still occurs; 'By – die' in the penultimate couplet; not the girl, surely, but the affair, for in September the singer remembers that the love 'has now grown old'.

Such a simple, short song demands music of the utmost simplicity. The alliteration of the lyric is echoed in the ostinato music, and the constant flow around the same key. This is a gem.

In the light of later developments the next song 'The Sounds Of Silence' is a most revealing performance. It begins slower than we expect, if we know the succeeding Simon and Garfunkel versions, and in general Simon is a little rougher with his song than he allowed it to be used later. Judith Piepe calls it 'a major work', the very phrase Art Garfunkel applies to it on his notes for the *Wednesday, 3 a.m.* album, and it must have created a vivid impact on listeners of twenty years ago. In many ways this performance senses the need for fuller treatment; Simon – or someone else – taps an insistent rhythm as the song grows in intensity; his voice becomes more urgent and compelling; the tempo is gradually increased and the guitar is heavily struck. It is as though the artist is about to burst the confines of his own resources, to tell the world of the certainty of his vision.

In the complete recorded legacy of Simon and Garfunkel this may not be the most profound version of the song, but on its own terms it provides an overwhelming experience.

And the result of ignoring the 'warning', of a lack of spiritual qualities to compensate for the avoidance of human contact? Self-obsession, selfishness, and profound loneliness that leads directly to an early death. The 'Most Peculiar Man' of the next song committed suicide by turning on the gas last Saturday. His neighbour, Mrs Reardon, tells us 'he was a most peculiar man'. The rock has crumbled, the island is submerged.

The song is therefore another warning against turning inwards upon oneself, and as Simon performs it in the most matter of fact way, rather like a court official reading the most awful details in a clinical, detached manner, the impact is the greater. More is achieved by the understatement here than by all the *angst* of public grief.

Art Garfunkel says in his liner note, 'He was my brother . . . the innocent voice of an uncomfortable youth'. This is well said, the immediate post-war generation having been brought up in the comparative safety of a Western world so shocked and exhausted by the horrors of world war that violence within it was almost burned out by the conflict. Fifteen or so years later, with swastikas daubed on synagogues in Germany, the natural aggression of man was exerting itself in frighteningly familiar ways, which were nevertheless new to the younger generation. So when Garfunkel speaks of 'uncomfortable youth' one senses the corruption of innocence, or as Henry James put it, 'The ceremony of innocence is drowned'. But the feeling of brotherly love, with a martyr to man's inhumanity to man, is a spiritual, life-enhancing one. The song, in spite of a certain squareness in its structure and less than inspired melody, met wide acceptance by the sympathetic youth of Simon's generation.

By all accounts the Kathy of 'Kathy's Song' was an English girl with whom Paul Simon had struck up a close personal relationship. The singer of this song is in New York: 'I gaze . . ., where my heart lies.' The actual cut of the melody appears to owe something to Dylan. The spirituality that has been such a surprising and consistent feature of the songs of this collection is reinforced by the

80

Art Garfunkel, 1972

A forthcoming UK appearance and European tour is announced,
London, April 1982

Even press conferences have their lighter side. US, 1983

In rehearsal, 1983

Together again, 1982

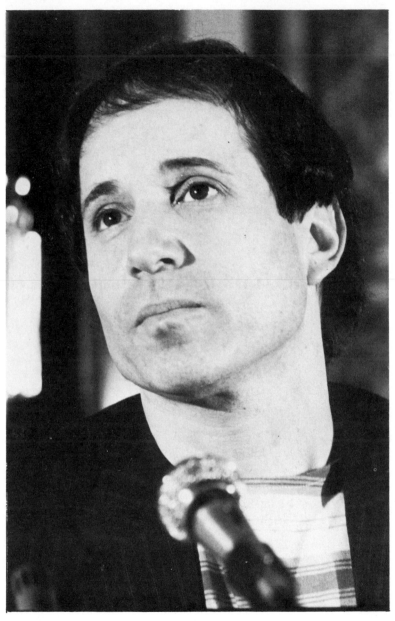

Paul Simon during a press conference, London, April 1982

oblique religious references to 'the only truth I know is you'. God is Love, Christ tells us, and as God is Truth also, as Gandhi told us, it follows that true love is more than a physical state. It may be too much to claim that in his love the singer senses spiritual qualities over and above those of his everyday life, but the fact that one can infer such things is a measure of this remarkable artist's achievement. At times one has to stop and remind oneself that this is music written within a popular framework.

In 'The Side Of A Hill' a child's corpse is buried; the soldier who killed him polishes a gun. Immediately, in the light of Simon and Garfunkel's later development, we connect with 'Scarborough Fair'. This is the first version (or at least an early one) of the 'Canticle' behind 'Scarborough Fair'.

One can understand the reasons for changing it. The imagery here is somewhat brutal and the experience not fully realized. The experience is also second hand, however well intentioned, but as an early draft for the later masterpiece it is worth the occasional airing.

'A Simple Desultory Philippic' also resurfaces on a later Simon and Garfunkel album, *Parsley, Sage, Rosemary and Thyme*, when Robert McNamara – President Johnson's Secretary for Defence, one of his three special advisers on the growing war in Vietnam and arguably the most disastrous of the trio – replaced Lyndon Johnson in the song's lengthy subtitle, 'Or How I Was Lyndon Johnsoned Into Submission'.

This song has already been described in the section on the *Parsley, Sage, Rosemary and Thyme* album. This performance, which preceded the other, is just as wry and perhaps the more genuine for being closer to the whole string of influences to which Simon refers and acknowledges have shaped his life. There are few surprises, for a sensitive literary young man of his

81

generation could hardly have remained aloof from them. Significantly, perhaps, the reference to Dylan is oblique and spoken, not sung, in Bob Dylan's own 'parlando' style, but the cross-reference to Dylan Thomas is also significant for literary reasons. The music spurts out and ejaculates, perfectly setting this early type of verbal collage.

'Flowers Never Bend With The Rainfall' is another song that appears on the *Parsley, Sage, Rosemary and Thyme* album. Here the music is moved to the centre stage, as the constant repetition of the same note demands a changing harmonic pattern to sustain it. Judith Piepe says it has a 'rain-soft' melody. The inherent gentleness and almost feminine qualities of this song are its most lasting characteristics. But the sentiment, summed up in the haunting line 'I'll continue to continue', is essentially optimistic, as hope springs eternal.

The final song on the album, 'Patterns', was also used on the later album. In this recording it comes over as an amazing song. Apart from its inherent qualities, which are considerable (the monotonality, the incessant minor mode and the narrow compass in which the melody moves, forcing the music into a tight band of concentration), its literary images sum up everything on the album. Night, birth, death, love, children, the lonely room, disappointment and uncertainty with the outside world, unyielding belief in the creative artist's spritual qualities and strength (the powers to overcome any obstacle) and the fundamental integrity of this solution are all here. It is fabulous, the more so for being heard in context – the patterns of this changing chiaroscuro defining a work of genius.

1971

PAUL SIMON
For track listings see Discography p. 152

A gentle reggae beat (*not* the beat of the late 1970s) nudges 'Mother And Child Reunion' into life. This is new – a totally different Paul Simon from the start. But this is no white man's reggae, no cheap imitation; Simon here takes the happy, moderately fast beat of reggae with the delicious short syncopated chords as a tapestry on which to weave one of his most attractive solo songs.

Simon says the song arose from contemplating the menu in a Chinese restaurant, a dish of chicken and eggs. To a literary mind such as his the implications must have been enormous; death, reunion, sex, Oedipus – any of which would have been totally out of place here. But the man does it. With sleight of hand, by subtle emphasis and innuendo, each of these myriad subjects is touched upon. And yet it is all done with the most infectious music, which has 'hit' written all over it. If ever artistic merit deserved success, this is it.

'Duncan' – we learn his name is Lincoln Duncan – is another major achievement. The singer takes on the persona of Duncan as he muses over his life one evening in a motel room. It is here: the first experience with a woman ('just like a dog', a sensational line), and a whole succession of images against a gently pulsating guitar accompaniment. It is New Mexico perhaps, for Los Incas, the ethnic group from *Bridge Over Troubled Water*, are the backing musicians. Their Mediterranean warmth adds a suitable haze which almost makes one curl up with pleasure. 'Everything Put Together Falls Apart' is a recitative-like song, the additional instruments contributing nothing. It would have been better to have recorded this in the manner of *The Paul Simon*

83

Songbook album. Spencer Leigh says: 'It meanders inconclusively and was clearly written for the message that you should control the drugs you take or they'll end up controlling you. A valid point, certainly, but not really substantial enough for a whole song.' While one can agree up to a point, in Simon's defence it should be pointed out that it is (at less than two minutes' playing time) the shortest song on side one and comes as a welcome aural relief from the varied instrumentation of the first two. But it is difficult not to agree with Leigh when he says 'the song is weak'. The comparatively crude presentation suggests that Simon felt it so himself.

A warning song to those who abuse their bodies (another of those 'dual' songs, following the previous one on a similar theme) is 'Run That Body Down'. This may seem a strange subject, but by this time we ought to realize that this artist can do almost anything in song. For him nothing is impossible in music. It has to be autobiographical (Spencer Leigh is convinced it is, with evidence for his belief), but a nice touch is that when he arrives home from the doctor, having been warned of the dangers, he repeats to his wife the doctor's warning. The implications are clear and of more than localized significance, even if the song remains less than first class. The performance is very fine, but one would have liked to have heard Garfunkel tackle the demanding high tessitura, which causes Simon's voice a few problems. Furthermore, although the harmonies are well worth the study of any musician, especially the harmonic progressions themselves, the melody does not warrant such close attention.

'Armistice Day' is another disappointing number, disjointed and fussily produced as if to compensate for its inherent weaknesses. As such this side ends with a feeling of letdown after the two brilliant songs with which it began. It lacks the unity of the best of his previous work, and the continuing memorability of the earlier masterpieces.

As if to answer these dubious thoughts, 'Me And Julio Down By The Schoolyard' bursts upon us as a perfectly realized piece of superb writing. A simple yet hauntingly effective guitar sound (with the lightest touches from the drums) on the left-hand channel are almost immediately joined on the right. Curiously, for a song which conjures up such a vivid image – of furtive teenage schoolyard sex, unwittingly observed by the girl's mother – the factual details are obscure. Simon admitted he did not know what it was the mother saw that was against the law, but the implications are clear. This light and breezy performance is most effective, and of such good humour that no one could possibly object to illicit, unlawful sex being treated as though it was insignificant. A deeper message is that if the letter of the law may have been broken it should always be tempered with mercy. 'Me And Julio . . .' is a tremendous achievement; few other singer–songwriters at this time could have brought off such a song, comprised of such apparently disparate elements, all formed into an indestructible creation.

Another splendid song, 'Peace Like A River', follows. This is magisterially performed. Without labouring the point, the anti-Vietnam movement, which like almost all postwar 'peace' movements tended to take in fellow travellers of less than impeccable honour, meant much more to Americans, of course, than to Europeans. This is not to say that Europeans could not feel equal revulsion at the nightly television news spectacles, but that the USA was more directly involved, and it was young Americans who were called upon to do the fighting, not old men. Bernard Shaw makes the point in *Heartbreak House* – 'old men are dangerous; it matters not to them what happens to the world' – yet maturity and experience cannot be acquired except by having done a whole variety of things.

The concept of peace, flowing like a river, irrigating men's consciousness and directing their actions, is essential to life. Without it the human race is finished, and yet in popular music such sentiments – however well-intentioned – are often the excuse for crude outbursts. Here Simon has produced a superb song, which in its irregularity itself flows 'like a river'. Nothing is recapitulated exactly, and the constant four in a bar against occasional triplets and wide-leaping intervals during the instrumental breaks make this a 'peace' song of thinking men.

A slow, gently rocking 3/4 introduction leaves one unprepared for the opening line of the following song, 'Papa Hobo': 'It's carbon and monoxide, the ole Detroit perfume.' The hobo has to leave Motown yet he has to use a vehicle to do it.

In the early 1970s the Detroit Tamla Motown record company was one of the most important in the world, with a whole string of hits each of which had a recognizable Tamla sound. Simon has achieved the remarkable feat of writing a song around the city without using any Tamla formulae. The basic, dirt-poor instruments – harmonium, acoustic guitar and bass harmonica – ideally create the right sound image. The harmonium is imaginatively used, played by Larry Knechtel, the pianist on *Bridge Over Troubled Water*. That, however, is about all the interest the track possesses, and the succeeding track, 'Hobo's Blues', for all its surprising qualities, is a corollary of it. On 'Hobo's Blues' (one of two songs on the album recorded in Paris – the other being 'Duncan') Paul Simon accompanies Stephane Grappelli's blues violin. Simon is no Django

Rheinhardt but he makes an excellent job. Curiously enough, as 'Hobo's Blues' is in the same key as that which ended the previous 'Hobo' song (but not that which began it – a rare example, but by no means the last, of Simon starting a song in one key and ending in another) it functions as an appendix, a jam version of some of the previous material. Grappelli plays well, displaying his customary virtuosity including a deliciously sliding A harmonic way up on the fingerboard, but should not the final cadence be in the minor mode, not the major that ends it? This is the only question mark against a rare fragment of fine music-making.

The growing threat to Tamla Motown records was the Philly Sound of Gamble and Huff in 1972. The O'Jays, a great black male harmony group in the Philly stable, had a sizeable hit that year with 'Back Stabbers'. This theme is echoed in 'Paranoia Blues'. The O'Jays sing: 'They smile in your face, all the time they want to take your place', and Simon sings: 'They'll smile right to my face, O when my back is turned they'd like to stick it to me . . .' There the resemblance ends, for this is a genuine blues, albeit of irregular bar and chord structure. The sound, of bottleneck guitar played by Stefan Grossman and percussion by Simon himself, is an ethnic one, pure folk in many ways, but a country blues and therefore less rigid than, say, Muddy Waters. The lyrics demand attention, not just because of the paranoia warning that people are likely to lose just about everything they possess in New York (a growing fact of life in the city then was the soaring street crime rate) but because of Simon's pliant use of words. The 'nick' of 'I just got out in the nick of time' also infers theft (not a third meaning, in British slang, of prison) and this theft (even of his food) occurs in the next verse.

Even so, the inherent pessimism of the song makes it

87

less than attractive, and the final number, 'Congratulations', picks up the theme of petty urban crime and turns it, amazingly, on its head, forcing us to feel nothing but sympathy for those so dispossessed that they have no alternative but to steal in order to live. It is more than that, a personal statement of damaged personal relationships. Leigh sums it up perfectly: '. . . Simon is melancholic over his society spawning so many divorces and his voice almost breaks with sadness as he asks his final question, whether peaceful coexistence is possible.' The final instrumental coda is bitter-sweet and fades, alone, on the right-hand channel, as Simon wanders off beyond our hearing.

1972

THERE GOES RHYMIN' SIMON
For track listings see Discography p. 152

'Kodachrome' bursts the album into life with irresistible force. This is an excellent track, well performed, extremely well produced and wholly infectious as a musical experience. What is uncertain, however, is whether the song divorced from the production trappings would be that good. But it is fascinatingly written in two keys, the dominant taking over from the tonic in the middle section to function as a second tonic. What this means for the non-technical reader is that at just the right moment the song jumps up five tones, and the sense of exhilaration is wholly refreshing. It comes a second time, and just at the point when one thinks the ace cannot be trumped Simon does just that by accelerating into the coda, doubling the speed in a dazzling display of virtuosity, and all tied together within a succession of rock and roll cells.

The track tingles with life, teeming with imaginative touches, from the startling use of the word 'crap' in the first line to the incessant little drum-like taradiddles way on the right. Here is a real aural imagination at work, and the result is a track of which any self-respecting musician would be proud.

With 'Tenderness', the second number, there is a heavy emphasis on 'production'. The clear, direct expression of *The Paul Simon Songbook* is light years away from this collage. Against a gospel background Simon sings a mildly interesting song immaculately, but it lacks true commitment. One gets the distinct impression that this highly talented musician is trying on this kind of arrangement because it seemed like a good idea at the time, not because the song demanded it. Such a track, thus arranged, would be ideal on a television special with a star-studded line-up, but the glutinous background detracts so much from the sentiment that it is in grave danger of lapsing into cloying sentimentality. This may be a new emotion on a Paul Simon record; it is an unwelcome one. The use of the Dixie Hummingbirds, an immensely respected gospel group, is an unnecessary extravagance, and however important they may be, in the last analysis their presence is neither here nor there.

In 'Take Me To The Mardi Gras' Simon goes to his top drawer. It is a lovely spectacle towards the end of siesta time as the moderately slow Iberian rhythms beguile and cajole the senses. So far, so good; we think we know where we are, epecially when a New Orleans Creole band (the Onward Brass Band) shuffles across the music like a collection of Pied Pipers leading us on. But Simon does not leave it at that; his vision demands a high voice. Regretting Garfunkel's absence, he employs the Rev. Claude Jeter to float above the music. This worthy gentleman was the lead singer of the Swan Silvertones, the very group that inspired 'Bridge Over Troubled Water'. The words here echo those of 'Bridge': 'lay my burden down', 'upon the shore' and 'wash' reflect the imagery of the earlier song in a subtle recollection.

Throughout this song we have observed the growing mastery of Paul Simon and his outward-looking creativity, which has occasionally (as on this record) taken him into areas where he is less successful. The constantly surprising thing about any musical genius is that it is constantly surprising; the next song, 'Something So Right' is a fabulous achievement, utterly original, unexpected yet amazing in its certainty of expression. It is one of the finest love songs of our time, and if that seems an extravagant claim, close analysis of the song demonstrates it beyond doubt. The uncertain tonal scheme of the introduction exactly mirrors the uncertainty of the singer, which is further echoed in the completely irregular bar phrases and bar lengths – 3/4, 4/4, 4/4, 2/4, 4/4, and so on, measures that would not be out of place in Stravinsky. But instead of producing a jerkiness, as may be inferred, the result is a halting, touching expression, like someone quietly feeling for the right words. The arrangement by Quincy Jones is wholly successful, and although it has upset some Simon enthusiasts it is difficult not to appreciate the artistry – to say nothing of the result this artistry has created – of the whole thing. Occasionally in popular music 'taste' and 'style' can almost be euphemisms for a kind of glutinous blandness and are often meaningless concepts in themselves, but these words come to mind in this superb achievement. The words show Simon at his best, and as they are fortunately reproduced on the album sleeve, had best be studied by the interested listener. The song does not reveal its qualities easily and the listener has to work to savour them, but the result is well worth the effort.

To cleanse our ears from the Mahlerian excesses of the previous song the pure sound of a descending piano sequence changes the image completely. 'One Man's Ceiling Is Another Man's Floor' is another of Simon's most effective songs, about a tenement house; the title says it all.

The theme of non-communication, of caring for others, is here, but the words are not as important as they are in other songs. Here the music is the most important feature, and the piano (beautifully played by Harry Beckett) has two identities. The descending smooth triplets are one, and the aggressive rising octave jazz-rock phrase is the other. The ceiling and the floor are here graphically drawn. The song is knowingly observed; Simon describes the whole situation in a nutshell and with music so appropriate that they fit like hand and glove. Indeed, in this regard this is a song worthy of the Gershwins, but they might have demurred over one of the longest fades in the catalogue.

When this album was released some surprise was expressed that the next song, 'American Tune', is based upon a Lutheran chorale used by J. S. Bach in his *St Matthew Passion*. Bach's masterpiece is one of the greatest expressions of the human mind in art. It dates from 1729, and during it Bach quotes several Lutheran chorales (a practice echoed by Michael Tippett in his *A Child Of Our Time*, though the 'popular' tunes are spirituals), with which the largely peasant class of the congregation would be familiar. But the chorale itself is not by Bach, nor is it by Martin Luther. In 1522 Luther changed the German Passion service, increasing the part played by the congregation and introducing German chorales (what today we would call hymns). The most famous of these is the Passion Chorale 'O Haupt, voll Blut und Wunden' (O Sacred Head, sore wounded), which Bach introduces five times in his *St Matthew Passion*.

Luther, in an attempt to get the message across, used earlier, popular tunes for the chorales, and this great melody quoted by Paul Simon is one of Europe's oldest known popular melodies, adapted for religious purposes but having its roots in folk music. Simon thus has every justification for using it for his own purposes, and the connection with Europe in the late Middle Ages (at the time America was discovered) is highly appropriate in this context.

Simon's song is a hymn too, but to America. It is not an anthem, but asks the question how a country founded upon such moral strength and of such admirable principles could have seemingly lost its way. Watergate was just around the corner.

In complete contrast, 'Was A Sunny Day', the mildly innocuous number that follows, infers the loss of her virginity by one Lorelei to a naval man named Earl. She ominously refers to him as 'Speedoo', which raises a number of unanswered questions. It would appear to have been a somewhat painless process, made easier by the idyllic surroundings of which the title describes only one. Maggie and Terre Roche provide the high voices Garfunkel would have provided in other circumstances; the distinguished percussionist Airto Moreira is somewhat wasted on the track, his contribution being no more noteworthy than that of any other self-respecting session musician. The locale is Newport News, a city near Norfolk, Virginia, at the mouth of the James River, but without such knowledge one might be forgiven for thinking it happened in the Caribbean.

The innocuous atmosphere continues in 'Learn How To Fall', a somewhat mundane song with few redeeming features. Indeed, it is hard to see what the song is about or what impelled Simon to write it. It is well done, in parts very well done, but it adds nothing to our perception.

'St Judy's Comet' is a quiet up-tempo lullaby for Simon's then infant son. Again, this song has no independent life outside the album, but it is nicely written and immaculately presented. It contains the deliciously self-deprecatory, 'If I can't sing my boy to sleep, well it makes your famous daddy look so dumb.' One should point out that three words are missing from the text on the sleeve at the end of verse seven.

'When I was a little boy' is the first line of the final song of the album, 'Loves Me Like A Rock'. Clearly this picks up the 'little boy' theme from the lullaby and turns it into something quite new. It is merely the starting point for a magnificent gospel setting of a curiously shaped song, 'My Mama Loves Me', repeated again and again, 'like a rock'. The song cross-refers to virtually every song on the album – in timbre 'Tenderness', 'Take Me To The Mardi Gras'; in imagery 'American Tune', 'Was A Sunny Day', 'St Judy's Comet'; and in literary allusiveness 'Learn How To Fall', 'Kodachrome' (where 'I've got a Nikon camera' in the earlier song becomes 'I've got the Presidential seal' in the latter). All this is unique in Simon's output, and the justification for using the Dixie Hummingbirds is complete in this brilliant setting, burning with the ringing affirmation of revivalist fervour.

1974

PAUL SIMON IN CONCERT –
LIVE RHYMIN'

For track listings see Discography p. 152

When this album was announced for release in the UK in 1974 considerable disappointment was expressed at the contents; the fifth album to include 'The Sounds Of

Silence', and others in similar versions, was thought to be stretching the loyalties of the Simon enthusiasts to the limit. Dealer reaction, too, was somewhat negative and it was difficult to get stores to stock an album that seemed to add nothing to previously over-recorded material. On the plus side was the generous playing time – over fifty-two minutes of music, making the album good value, but the sleeve is poor and lacks information.

Furthermore, the tour from which these tracks came was itself originally undertaken to promote the *Rhymin' Simon* album, and a general feeling of *déja vu* can well be imagined. It is not easy to bring off a tour to promote an album and then record the tour for release as a live album, but against all the odds it worked.

The first thing that impresses is that it is basically the Paul Simon of his first solo album – just a singer with his guitar, and later with a handful of picked instrumentalists and singers. There is none of the massive stage managed hyper-gigs of the time, but a return to a pure and unfettered approach. This brings rewards immediately in the first song, 'Me And Julio Down By The Schoolyard', where the accumulated accompaniment of the earlier version is cleaned away. We can appreciate the song for what it is and how Simon himself must have played it when it was fully formed in his mind. The effect is delicious, and is heightened by some fine whistling from Simon in place of the instrumental break. 'Homeward Bound', which follows, is an acknowledgement of those roots; this is another marvellous performance, full of atmosphere, and was well worth issuing for it adds something that one felt was destroyed by the original recording. The 'American Tune' also gains immeasurably by this treatment, and as it is almost the earliest and purest folk-type tune on which Simon has based any of his numbers, one can clearly

94

sense the ethnic qualities, especially as it is exceptionally well recorded. This could pass for a studio take (apart from the obligatory – but mercifully few – audience noises). The first disappointment is 'El Condor Pasa'. Simon is joined by Urubamba, descended from Los Incas, but the balance between his voice and the pipes on the left-hand channel is poor. The wind sound is too loud and the ensemble tentative. The audience effectively ruins our enjoyment, for they are impelled to applaud not only when the song starts but also when Simon starts singing. Urubamba's playing is unconvincing and disappointingly feeble, leaving Simon having to work hard to get them to swing, but the audience was in an uncritical frame of mind. 'Duncan' is the second of the three consecutive songs with Urubamba and again the audience is childishly infuriating, but this is a good performance, much better than 'El Condor Pasa' and a viable alternative to the studio version on the *Paul Simon* album. 'The Boxer' completes the Urubamba set and the first side. The ethnic instrumentation suits the song very well, particularly as they take over the 'lie-la-lie' section. The only moment that disappoints is the lack of a sharp 'cut him' in the final verse. The little C major instrumental tune works better here than on the *Bridge Over Troubled Water* album, and the inclusion of an additional chorus not on the original version is a substantial bonus, even without a printed text.

Side two begins with Simon introducing the Jessy Dixon Singers, whose line-up is shown on the photograph at the foot of the back of the sleeve. 'Mother And Child Reunion' is the first number, and it is not good. Ensemble is again ragged, as it was with the first Urubamba song, and the beat drags. The hand-claps are so feebly recorded they have to be heard to be believed, and the organ is insensitively played. The album would have been much improved by the omission of this track, which all but destroys this great song.

As the song ends the atmosphere grows suddenly quiet and mysterious; the sound of silence descends over the auditorium and this very song now follows. The female trio of Jessy Dixon Singers join with Simon to make an unexpectedly moving and vibrantly flawless re-creation of this masterpiece. Jessy Dixon himself sings verse three as a solo, and the transfiguration is complete. Hypnotic and timeless, nothing can stop the magisterial procession of this great number.

'Jesus Is The Answer' is given over to the Jessy Dixon Singers; Simon is absent, and it is a very moving performance of its type. Simon returns for 'Bridge Over Troubled Water', but the song suffers from the lack of a piano. Because this crucial instrument is absent the audience sits in stupefaction, unable to recognize what the guitar chords portend until Simon begins the first verse, whereupon the atmosphere is ruined by spontaneous applause. Simon sings his own creation exceptionally well, and the recording is technically outstanding for a live album. The handful of musicians on stage forces some drastic reinstrumentation (no synthesizer keyboard was used) but it works so well that any initial doubts are completely dispelled, helped by a tempo that is judged to a nicety. The ending, most surprisingly, is quiet compared with the massive tumult that ended the original version, but it works very well with a total lack of pomposity.

'Loves Me Like A Rock' from the *Rhymin' Simon* album is a natural for this occasion, and as a live performance it has much to offer. The immediacy and the occasional spontaneous flicks are hugely enjoyable; it is difficult to keep one's feet still while listening to this track.

Finally, 'America', and back five years to the *Bookends* album. It is Simon alone again with his guitar. Video would have explained what is happening on stage during this generally fine performance, for something appears to amuse the audience, which applauds and cries out at incongruous moments. Eventually even the jerks are won over by Simon's genuine performance and lapse into hushed acceptance as the old images pass by, now honed by our experiences.

In sum, this album confounded those critics who tended to dismiss it without giving it a chance. It adds greatly to our appreciation of Paul Simon both as a composer and as a performer, and the Simon discography would be very much the poorer had it not been released.

1975

STILL CRAZY AFTER ALL THESE YEARS
For track listings see Discography p. 152

The title track, correctly the opening for side one, is a winner. It is splendidly performed and its knowing expression is attractively self-deprecatory. It is, however, much more than a self put-down; the music is a distinct advance on Simon's previous harmonic thinking. Musicians, knowing that the song begins with the flat supertonic and slides into the tonic (with an added sixth as the main melody note) at the first entry of the voice and ends firmly in the supertonic itself, will be aware that something highly unusual is afoot. Non-musicians will not be able to name what is happening, but their ears will tell them that strange stirrings are under way. The harmonies under the tune are riveting in their wide spectrum; listen to what happens at the second appearance of the word 'years' at the end of verse one.

Nothing remotely like this (technically the minor subdominant where the tonic should be) has been heard in Paul Simon's music up to this time. Our ears are stretched, our interest quickened, but without stress or ill-temper, and at all times the material is controlled by a slow, insidious 3/4 pulse and cushioned by Bob James's highly imaginative arrangement, which is discreet and highly appropriate.

The feeling of the passing of time is further enhanced by the appearance of none other than Art Garfunkel on the next track, 'My Little Town'. Far from bringing back rose-tinted memories, all sweetness and The Waltons, it is a somewhat detached view, not without a certain bitterness, as though worldly experience has taught the artist that small-town virtues are meaningless in the cut and thrust of the big city.

Musically it exhibits more of Simon's growing harmonic daring. A glance at the music – published in *The Paul Simon Complete* book – will show the musician this evolutionary (not revolutionary) change of style, and the sympathetic non-musician's ears will tell him the differences, with unusual yet curiously appropriate harmonies underpinning the melody and subtly disconcerting changes of pulse and metrical scansion. Yet in spite of all this sophistication the song lacks memorability, lacks the direct certainty of Simon's earlier work.

'I Do it For Your Love' continues in this vein. Nor are we saddened by Garfunkel's absence, for Simon's double-tracking more than compensates. The harmonies are even more unusual, following the very chromatic melody like a cat until eventually one begins to wonder if the composer can remember what key he is supposed to be in. In musical terms the theme of the song – the breakdown of his marriage – is achieved by this extremely fluid harmonic state, yet the song smacks a little of self-righteousness. It becomes almost an anti-feminine statement, leaving a slightly bitter taste in the mouth. One sympathizes with Simon's personal problems, but is it not a little arrogant to write a whole string of songs about them, spend an enormous amount of money on recording them, and then expect wide public acceptance of the results? It carries the same connotations as Richard Strauss writing a large symphonic poem about himself and calling the result 'A Hero's Life'. Not everyone who is married is unhappy, and Simon treads a thin layer of ice at this point.

However, his growing compositional mastery answers these strictures in the next song, '50 Ways To Leave Your Lover', which pulls him back from the brink of morbid self-pity. This is expressed with a deft, light touch without any straining after effect. The chorus is nicely boppy, mature and without rancour, maybe the best of all ways. It is a good song, genuinely put across and perhaps more typical of Simon's true feelings than the earlier syrup. Even those who do not share his sentiments could hardly fail to respond to the attractive musical features and the nicely paced vocals.

'Night Game' is well described by Patrick Humphries with the word 'inscrutable'. It is certainly that and seems deliberately to avoid any pleasant or attractive features. Death, winter, night, failure and a deep, low tonality – all these chill the bones and the song is to be avoided at all costs if one is feeling depressed, so suicidal is its black vision. And yet it ends in the major mode.

Having brought us down with him at the end of side one, Simon immediately grasps us by the scruff of the neck at the start of side two with 'Gone At Last'. Picking up the wintry theme of 'Night Game', he transforms it into a fast gospel number of high quality. With outstanding piano work from Richard Tee, and with the Jessy Dixon Singers in the background, Simon duets with the appropriately named Phoebe Snow, whose fabulous voice is heard first as a fine solo in the second verse and with Simon in verse three. Her soft, ecstatic high notes at the end are magnificent. The 'Gone At Last' is not Simon's marriage but the singer's 'string of bad luck', a situation probably familiar to all of us.

'Some Folks' Lives Roll Easy', however, Simon's next song, correctly divines that such fortunate people are in the minority. In an unusual collection this stands apart; against a vestigial trace of country blues Simon talks to God on a personal level as man to man, a specifically Judaic touch. Sad to say, Simon's own string arrangement in the song detracts from, rather than enhances it; he adds a simple violin line that would have benefited – assuming it had to be there in the first place – from some harmony. Ultimately this is not one of Simon's happier creations.

But happiness – or rather hedonism – is the theme of 'Have A Good Time', the best song on the album, which comes next. It flows with all the old naturalness, yet it is in 7/4 (two bars, one of 4/4, followed by one of 3/4) in the verse followed by a sliding, overtly promiscuous 4/4 chorus. The song is full of sexuality and also materialism, and it is unforgettably sleazy. A raving unaccompanied saxophone solo freewheels the song to an end in an amazing way.

'You're Kind' is a surprisingly original song, inexplicable in the context. The sensitive, compassionate young man of The Paul Simon Songbook is here replaced by an uncaring, selfish individual who is more interested in his own comfort than the feelings of others, even someone close to him to whom he owes much. This is no moral tract; whatever the singer does is his affair and no

100

one else's, except when he makes it public and invites our approval. If this is the result of the hedonism of the previous song, then we have a fifty-first way to leave our lover. The final song, 'Silent Eyes', is a disturbed and disturbing statement. 'Silent eyes watching Jerusalem' is the opening phrase of the lyric. Jerusalem is a holy city for three religions: Judiasm, Christianity and Islam. It is too simplistic, surely, to think of this as Simon's Jewish testament. Religion has been a recurring theme in his work and it is natural to turn to it in times of stress. This song is surely about man's inhumanity to man; no one will comfort Jerusalem, the beleagured city, Simon seems to be saying, she 'weeps alone'. The music is hardly up to the level of this important theme but the song does have a geninely moving impact. An extended piano solo (very well played by Leon Pendarvis) takes us away from such thoughts, leaving the singer and his words, and threads its curious way back to the minor mode, with the mediant discarded. This is the same chord that ends 'The Sounds Of Silence', and with it Simon effectively draws a discreet silence over his recording career for five years.

1977

GREATEST HITS, ETC.
For track listings see Discography p. 153

This unusually titled album is nothing more than what it says; the 'etc.' is made up of two previously unreleased songs. They are splendid, and the first, 'Slip Slidin' Away', is one of Simon's best. It harks back to the early 1970s, before the *Still Crazy* album, because it lacks the touches of self-indulgence, of faint pretension, that on occasion mar that curious document. Furthermore, the harmonies, although by no means predictable, are more

101

logical and move with greater certainty. The song, too, has a much wider relevance than most of the *Still Crazy* items. Although the basic tempo is quite slow, a quietly persistent beat gives the song a dual rhythmic aspect, intriguing in effect. Simon's voice is in excellent shape and is beautifully recorded in just the right perspective. The old alliterations trip off the tongue with delightful fluency, and the Oak Ridge Boys, a fine gospel quartet, add warm harmonies.

'Stranded In A Limousine' begins as a funky piano concerto before the tight vocal line declares this to be another great number. It is tremendous: brilliantly observed, poetical, laconic and deftly tongue in cheek, expressed in a surprisingly (for this composer) medium up-tempo funky style. One listens with growing pleasure to the scene of a wealthy individual stuck in his limousine in a broken-down neighbourhood. The instrumentation is a delight and the credit on the sleeve for arranging shows that it is Simon's own work. These two songs come as a great relief after the excesses of the *Still Crazy* album, and it is a pity that Simon did not have enough material for a brand new album along these lines, which would have been outstanding.

As it is, we have a greatest hits compilation, which the sleeve implies Simon had a hand in choosing. Whether he did or not, with no less than three songs from the previous album, whoever made the choice strains the English language – 'hits' indeed. Nearly all the tracks have been issued before and comments on them will be found in the discussion of the relevant album, but CBS could have exercised more care in the presentation of this product. Anyone with half an ear can hear that the 'Duncan' track is a live performance, but the sleeve information is stupidly wrong, reprinting the label copy credits from the 1971 *Paul Simon* album, a studio performance. The audience applause and extraneous noise proves that it comes from the *Live Rhymin'* album of 1974. It is Urubamba, therefore, not Los Incas, who should be credited, and the engineer is Phil Ramone, not Bernard Estardy and Roy Halee. Similarly the version of 'American Tune' is live but is not that of the *Live Rhymin'* album, for it includes a small string section. The label says it was first published in 1974; one would like to know where, for this performance has not appeared on any of the other albums discussed in this book.

With over fifty-one minutes playing time this album is good value, but not everyone will agree with the choice.

1980

ONE-TRICK PONY
For track listings see Discography p. 153

This album is a collection of the songs Simon wrote for the film *One-Trick Pony*, the *magnum opus* that had occupied him for a long time. This is not, therefore, a soundtrack album and is not offered as such. Because of this any strictures on the material have to be seen in this light, though with an artist of Simon's stature one expects the material to stand up on its own and not to require the prop of an outside event.

'Late In The Evening' is a bright, East-coast, up-tempo number with a buoyant, rhythmic drive and tight yet not blaring brass work. Against this fluent background Simon recalls times in his life 'late in the evening' (the times, not the recollection). He muses over when he was a baby (hearing his mother's laughter); as a boy out with the boys (*a capella* – i.e. unaccompanied – singing groups on the street corner); as a young musician (the music he played) and the first time he made love to his girl (with the music outside the room 'seeping through'). It is a

103

mature, thoughtful, fine song, brilliantly performed and recorded, yet it is not the music of youth.

'That's Why God Made The Movies' is a cool contrast, full of fascinating icy sounds in the middle distance, which act like an aural halo around Simon's closely miked and gentle voice. It has a dual tempo; one is slow to medium, the other reasonably fast, the two always held together to produce an other-worldly, distanced effect, admirably suited to the singer's purpose. It is a difficult song to appreciate fully, even with a knowledge of the film, and doubly so without it. The imagery is opaque and full of seemingly conflicting illusions that only heighten the weird atmosphere it inhabits.

'One-Trick Pony' is one of two live recordings on the album (the other being 'Ace In The Hole'). It is a very smooth, immaculate song, with an intelligent lyric and a super-smooth delivery. But it is so innocuous in effect that, divorced from the film, it has little significance or drive of the kind that forces the listener to pay attention. Though this song is doubtless sincere, sincerity, as Stravinsky said, 'is a *sine qua non* which guarantees nothing'.

A superlative poem distinguishes 'How The Heart Approaches What It Yearns'. It is allied to an upholstered musical setting to which no lover of background music could possibly object, and the melody is immediately forgettable. This is a tragedy, and the succeeding song, 'Oh, Marion' is another that seems to come from the same amnesiac stable.

The remaining songs on this album are couched in similar vein; 'Ace In The Hole' (the other live recording) is in two parts that do not add up to much. It is all very pleasant and professional, and at a purely technical level it is head and shoulders above the vast majority of popular music performances. But it merely goes through the motions, and never takes flight.

The same, regrettably, is true of 'Nobody' and 'Jonah'. The Paul Simon enthusiast must be bitterly disappointed by this collection, so bland and unvaried, such a pale imitation of past glories, however immaculately it is presented.

'God Bless The Absentee' is marginally more interesting, if only for the nice piano part. The strings and horns are redundant and never mix properly with the electric guitar (they rarely do anyway), but it is all a question of degree. With the best will in the world it is difficult not to be amazed that Simon appears satisfied with this collection of songs and the same-sounding, antiseptic arrangements. 'Long, Long Day' curdles like a bedtime drink commercial; with this malted milk Paul Simon's *One-Trick Pony* comes to an end.

1983

HEARTS AND BONES
For track listings see Discography p. 153

Those admirers of Paul Simon who had been disappointed by the less than compelling nature of his previous *One-Trick Pony* album had their faith in this artist's creative ability triumphantly reinforced by *Hearts and Bones*. Whilst not being a flawless masterpiece, it is possibly Paul Simon's finest solo album. It begins with the song 'Allergies'. This is a magnificent song, thrilling in its scope and impact, profoundly musical and original and showing Simon's genius undimmed by the passing of the years.

The most immediately striking aspect of *Hearts and Bones* is the album's virtually unique sound-world. 'Allergies' at once plunges us into this aural wonderland when it begins with a high oscillating electronic haze, airily fascinating like a half-perceived image just out of reach. A curious additional sound, the word 'maladies' intoned as if by a spatial droid, is now immediately joined by Simon, centimetres from the microphone, who turns 'maladies' to 'melodies' and, meandering through the fabric of the music until 'remain', the phrase's final word, ends on a long high note, floating as a cirrus cloud aloft in the sky.

Suddenly, banishing this reverie, a medium-soft rock rhythm is here, with additional drums flickering from right to left three times across the sound-image, reinforcing the cadence, the harmony, and pumping life into the music in great coital waves. Against this infectious rhythm the singer bemoans his lack of creativity (a reference perhaps to the *One-Trick Pony* failure?): "my hand can't touch a guitar string' which he blames on his current allergy to women, which is having some doubtful physical side-effects. But one thing is certain about this song: the words are on a very high level of inspiration, as anyone who takes the trouble to study them on the album's inner bag will conclude. Over and above this achievement and creating the most immediate impact is the supreme quality of the musical invention, which places this song among Simon's best since he split with Garfunkel – which is saying a lot. 'Allergies' has a magnificent production feel to it, and yet it is all handled with such care and sensitivity that one is never aware of production for production's sake. The music tingles with life and invention, and has that marvellous quality of expectation which keeps us eager to learn what is coming next, whatever it might be, and which continually surprises and delights us. Once again with this artist, this brilliance – for such it is – is not flung at the listener in a virtuosic sense, causing us to gasp at the physical impact of the sound as if we were witnessing an Olympic champion in full flight; no, this profoundly musical creativity has the intuitive feeling of something which one recognizes almost by instinct, and yet which of course did not exist before one's initial experience of it. This is a quality of art at its finest which this song clearly possesses in its own medium.

Some examples of the purely musical expressions of this genius can be found first in the song itself – that part of 'Allergies' in which Simon sings. To reinforce the words, to draw attention to their meaning, he adopts some surprising characteristics. Suddenly, the backing tracks will be cut off, as though there is an unexpected power cut, and momentarily we are left dangling in the air, sustained only by the abrupt immediacy of the singer, continuing in spite of the brief absence of accompaniment. This gesture (which occurs in slightly altered form on other songs in this album) might conceivably be one to remind the listener that nothing can be taken for granted. Another splendidly musical use of the accompaniment to reinforce the words is the repetition of a falling three-note and three-chord figure, once again using the heavy drums which blotted out the introduction (now, with growing realization, the obliteration of the word 'remain'). These occur around the phrase, which is only used on a couple of occasions, 'something's living on my skin'.

But the two main guitar breaks in the song – almost literally – break up the fabric of it, and paradoxically both concentrate our minds on the musical character of the song and at the same time, by their dazzling brilliance, utterly repudiate the opening bemoaning viewpoint: 'my hand can't touch a guitar string' indeed! These two extended solos, by Al Di Meola are breathtaking in their impact, recalling the supreme virtuosity of Gordon Giltrap. And yet, like Giltrap at his best, these solos do not just dazzle us with their feats of prestidigitation –

107

they are infinitely more subtle than that. The first, growing from the obsessive nature of the words in the opening part of the song, centres upon one note, repeated again and again in a kaleidoscopic phrase which worms its way at incredible speed around the one note: it is almost like the musical equivalent of a germ or bug, reproducing itself at a colossal rate and of course absolutely right for the musical personification of 'allergies', to say nothing of Simon's continuing verbal allusions to 'skin', 'doctor', 'maladies' and so on. The second solo is both the natural successor and complete musical opposite of the first. On the one hand, it is music – continuing the previous allusions – bursting with activity, seemingly unstoppable in a feverish animation which St Vitus would have adored. Indeed, it is virtually impossible for anyone listening to this second solo not to feel an irresistible urge to get up and dance, so powerful is this music's impact. And yet the jerky phrases – like an absurd funky Webern – cry out for 'break' choreography, or aerobic interpretation without a seamless flow. This toe-tapping music, on the other hand, is completely opposite from the single-note obsession of the first solo. It starts now with a pure rising fifth – a large interval on the guitar, driven bluesward by the subsequent imprint of the tonality's minor third, but again picking up on the sudden breaks in the sound which was such a feature of the earlier accompaniment. This amazingly brilliant conception is brought off with superb aplomb, and one can only register one's surprise and disappointment at the British company's decision not to issue this as the statutory single when the album was released.

The words, as mentioned earlier, also deserve comment, but there again one can spend hours pondering over their subtle and interlinking construction. The singer has a dual *persona*: he is both the observer and the

108

observed, but such is Simon's quality as a writer of lyrics that he sparks off many more ideas than perhaps he means to, and it is only when one hears this song in context with the others on the album that one gradually comes to realize that, in a variety of ways, each song is both independent of, and linked to, its predecessors and successors. One final piece of subtlety with 'Allergies': it ends, as it began, not with the tintinnabulous cascade of the opening, but in the air, cut off again, with a faintly ringing echo as the music suddenly fades out of our experience.

In the next song, 'Hearts and Bones', Simon continues the obvious physical connection but introduces another of his themes from the 1970s – his Jewish consciousness, openly, in the first line: 'One and one-half wandering Jews', omitting the million, but perhaps deliberately so, implying the age-old search for the promised land of the people, and reducing it to a personal, one-to-one basis. But this is a sleight-of-hand, for the music could not be further away from Israel if it could choose for itself. Another lifelong pet subject, that of Central America, and more especially the Hispanic Northern part, surfaces, with the naturally logical use of the acoustic guitar. The sound-world here is clearly a Southern-Mexican one, but the Jewish consciousness is immediately juxtaposed with the Catholic tradition of the area 'Blood of Christ Mountains of New Mexico'. A duality, then; the duality of the singer of the first song; the duality of a couple who are both individuals and conjoined to form one, via, of course their 'Hearts and Bones'. It is an amazingly subtle concept for a rock musician – although 'rock' as it has come to be known is largely absent from the diffused haze of the hot equatorial regions. That this is indeed the region is confirmed by the myriad traceries of the music: one could be lazing in the shade, aware of scorching sun a few feet away, and idly watching the fast-moving patterns of insects' wings, faintly out of focus in one's sight as one is too lazy to get them into proper perspective, but all taking place against the background of a still, dusty, unpeopled vista. Conversely, the hyper-activity on the surface acts as a cooling agent, like that of a fan, and the song proceeds on three levels at the same time: the first, slow-moving bass harmonies, like the outline of the unchangeable distance; secondly, the hyper-activity of the higher-stringed and percussion instruments with their continuous changes of pattern; and lastly, the singer, whose tempo is somewhere between the two, languidly meandering above the accompaniment, faintly anonymously at first, but that only because the punch line of the song – the revelation that it is, in fact, about a human relationship (that may well have taken place before, and given rise to, the 'Allergies' of the opening song). That one can imagine such connections between these songs is because of the adoption here of those occasional surprises in the first song: the sudden use of *a cappela* (unaccompanied) voices and the use of an echoing phrase, repeated loop-like, over and over again as it slowly fades in the distance at the same time as the song itself continues. The image of a man quietly repeating, drone-like, his opinion to his partner who is unable or unwilling to understand what it is he is trying to say is amazing, an effect that Verdi or Britten would have enjoyed.

To be able to speak of 'Hearts and Bones' in this manner betokens the song's qualities, but in the last analysis the personal nature of the lyric does not transfer well to a broader appeal. Consequently, for all its superb qualities, not all of which have been mentioned, this song lacks the immediacy of the first, a realization that here is a piece of music that simply *had* to be written. The

110

experience and skill, and the genuine manner of expression with which Simon communicates are admirable and exceptional qualities in the field of popular music.

The next song, 'When Numbers Get Serious' almost comes as a moment of relief (not that the two previous songs were particularly solemn, far from it), especially when the play on words is more light-hearted though no less subtle. The 'numbers' could be figures, or beats, or – more likely – girls. The central American atmosphere of the previous song moves eastwards to the West Indies, and has a more urban ethnic minority feel to it. Curiously, Lennon and McCartney's 'Ob-La-Di' song from the 1960s is recalled in its half-remembered blue-beat rhythm. The singer is further back from the microphone, leading one to assume that the words need not be taken too seriously – but certainly they should not be discounted. Here Simon is in his literary element: the plays on words, the Hopkins-like repetitions of syllables or short words just for the sound they create hark back to his very earliest work, and the fun way he will throw in another aspect of the subject – not just for effect – is a delicious demonstration of his unique qualities. Again, just when one thinks one has this song all tied up, he will introduce a new element; it may be a sudden 'dead acoustic', recalling again the earlier breaks in the sound from 'Allergies' and 'Hearts and Bones' and giving thereby the feeling of continuity we noted earlier, or a new character, in this case the girl: 'serious numbers will always be heard', tied in with the bubbling references to numbers (the great line in this context 'I will love you innumerably'). At the very end of the song, Simon reduces the numbers from four, to three, to two and finally to one, a clear reference to the line in 'Allergies' ('You take two bodies and you twirl them into one'), and a passing acknowledgement of the one-and one-half

111

of 'Hearts and Bones'. There can surely be few musicians of this creative calibre working in the world today.

The song 'Think Too Much' is a curious one, for there are two 'versions' on this album. More puzzlingly, apparently the second (at least, it is termed (b)) comes first – the one called (a) is on the other side of the record. Like a parallelogram, 'Think Too Much (b)' – what a title – reflects the pulse, if not the rhythm, of 'Hearts and Bones' and forms a fine rhythmic and aural contrast to 'When Numbers Get Serious'. It begins with another puzzling sound: one has to ask 'what is it?' and one never can be really sure, for it is like a sheep bleating, in time, of course, but the sound is ever so slightly varied: it does not seem to be always the same, as a complicated drum pattern – underneath this almost human whining – engages our musical interest before the singer enters. It could be a baby crying, but whatever it is, it is animate, incoherent, and seems to demand our sympathy. The tempo is very slow, with much restless fluctuation from the myriad percussion instruments on top. Gradually, as with the 'droid' from 'Allergies', this echoing cry becomes more human when Simon begins. It is another Mexican atmosphere, reinforcing the ABAB pattern of mood in this album by way of reference to 'Hearts and Bones'. But the opening words declare this to be very much an autobiographical song: 'The smartest people in the world, Had gathered in Los Angeles, To analyze our love affair, And finally unscramble us' (the words Simon sings, although these differ from those printed on the album's inner bag). The hook line is constantly repeated: 'Maybe I think too much', which, if this is indeed the case, would cause a rueful smile to flit across the singer's face, and implies that we – as listeners – ought not to take it too seriously. We should *not*, for musical reasons, as the song is quite short, for all its having long bass pedal

112

points which hold it, unable to float free by itself, firmly to the ground: an inescapable marriage, fate at work? Who knows: maybe we think too much.

The first side of this remarkable album ends with 'Song About the Moon', a great song and one of the best Simon has written for many years. Continuing the interlinking nature of the material on this album, it recalls, as did 'When Numbers Get Serious' the rhythms of popular music of a generation or so before. Here it is not the 1960s which are evoked but the late 1950s, for the rhythmic background to this song is that of a medium-tempo soft-rock country beat of 1958. The quality of this song lies less with the music than with the words, which are outstanding, and the slovenly, easy-going dragging beat, insistent but not overpowering is a perfect foil to the lyric. It is almost impossible to do justice to Simon's verbal achievement here: within the first five lines the allusions of 'moon', 'craters', 'alien', 'gravity' are clear enough, but astonishingly, these connections are nothing to do with the song or the subject. This remarkable song is about song-writing, and the final command 'Then Do It' is nothing more than a kick up the backside for a lazy artist – perhaps that self-same allergic person whose hands could not touch a guitar string in the album's opening track. But before then, Simon has taken us on a remarkable journey. In what one might call traditional popular music terms, 'moon' almost always rhymed with 'June', and the equation equalled 'love', but the 'June night' – the use of the word 'night' crucial in the context as well as forming another link with 'moon' – of this particular song comes immediately after a startling reference to an exploding pistol. Summer riots? An assassination? The exploding heart 'like a pistol on a June night' is immediately turned completely round: '. . . if you want to write a song about the heart . . . write a song

113

about the moon.' Such literary quality is endlessly fascinating. The third segment (after 'Moon' and 'June') brings in the word 'photograph' in an attempt to advise the would-be song-writer on how to write a song about a face. This reference, and its importance, is only revealed in the songs on the second side, but a backward glance to the earlier songs here is the previously-mentioned command 'then do it' – a corollary of 'thinking too much', when nothing gets done. It may not also be too fanciful to assume that this song effectively chronicles the crisis of confidence which might have followed the comparative failure of *One-Trick Pony*.

The intertwining links between the songs of side one might lead some readers into thinking that this album is a 'concept' or 'thematic' one. It most certainly is not – or if it is, it is by no means apparent. Almost any adept songwriter can string together a series of songs on or around the same subject; that, by itself, means very little, and whilst a great many important albums have been the result of such a concept, there are very few indeed like this album which, on close analysis and after prolonged listening, exhibit features of integrated contrasts, thematic development, organic unity, cross-fertilisation of ideas and their growth, which lead to the conclusion that one is in the presence of a master-artist, which, in music terms, means he has created a cycle of songs of almost symphonic sweep and cohesion. If this seems extravagant praise, then one can only point to the music itself, demonstrating that artistically the proof of the pudding is in the eating.

Nor is this characteristic a recent development in Simon's art: as we have noted, this has been observable in embryonic terms from his earliest work as a songwriter. Now, the mature and experienced artist can obviously – if he is so minded – create infinitely more subtle and finely-constructed pieces than the raw and comparatively inexperienced teenager. The problem faces – indeed, we all face it – is that in the teeming world of contemporary popular music such artistry is very likely to get swamped by the sheer amount of music competing for our attention. In some ways, that has always been the lot of a creative artist – nor is this a euphemism for the 'prophet without honour', for Simon's earlier success guarantees an audience for what he does, making him better placed than most – and there is always the likelihood that, in choosing to do other things, or even attempting an increased range of expression, the result might be artistically worthless. Even the greatest composers and musicians have found this, often to their cost, but the strength of the artist of genius is that he can learn from mistakes made whilst consciously seeking such a change, and use such fresh experience to create subsequent work, possessing those qualities with which he was previously unable to transfuse and transform his work.

During the mid to late 1970s Simon's work became faintly obsessed with a kind of self-pitying regard, possibly as a result of personal pressures, which was not altogether the healthiest direction his work could have taken. *One-Trick Pony* was, in retrospect, the furthest point he travelled along this particular road, and the result must have led to a reappraisal of his own position. Many artists would have given up at that point, have collapsed in a morass of self-indulgent recrimination – and some, in similar circumstances, have clearly done this. It speaks volumes for Simon's inner strength of character, which we have noted on several occasions before, that he could come back after such a disappointment with this wonderful album, so musical, intelligent, witty and tender.

The songs on side two are more varied than those on

115

the first: at least, that is their initial impression. As so often with Simon, such initial impressions are by no means everything, and the 'symphonic cycle' nature of the album is reinforced by the (a) version of 'Think Too Much' which opens the next group. The tempo is fast, unlike that of the previously heard (b). It is a more positive opening, welcome after the self-analysis of the concluding songs on side one, but the most startling musical innovation – at least for Simon – is the sudden impetuous reiteration of one note, in fast semi-quavers (sixteenth-notes), each finger-picked and brilliantly vibrant. Here, it seems, he takes the first guitar solo from 'Allergies' and turns the obsession with one note completely on its head; it burns itself into the brain in an extraordinary gesture of reconstruction. The song ends with the same words 'maybe I think too much' which ended the first version, but the music is not the same; Simon has at least exorcized this particular fiend, and he can move through his material, sympathetically observing all manner of things and events and commenting upon them as he sees fit, but no longer obsessed beyond measure.

An early theme of Simon's – that of travel – is clearly in 'Train in the Distance'. There is a background of rail travel, the familiar insistent throb and gentle rhythm, more akin to Villa-Lobos's 'The Little Train of the Caipira' in his Bachianas Brasilieras No 2 than in Honegger's more powerful 'Pacific 231'. Against the background of trains, then, the song unwinds, but as it does so one realizes that – his new-found objectivity to the fore – it is an encapsulated autobiographical song, nothing less than Simon's own first marriage and the birth of his son, the falling apart of the parents, their tual separation and subsequent life. Previously in his work this would have unleashed an emotionally anguished

116

stretch of music, but here he can view it reasonably objectively, as a fact of life, no longer something to get worked up about. But this experience is used as the format by which Simon reveals possibly the single most important thought about his own life and work, and treats it almost as a throw-away at the end of the song: 'What is the point of this story, What information pertains, The thought that life could be better, Is woven indelibly, Into our hearts and our brains.' This is it: this is Paul Simon's testament, and because of the supreme artist he is, it is done with myriad cross-references, most clearly by the correlation between the song's final words 'our hearts and our brains' and the title of the album from which it comes, *Hearts and Bones*. The betterment of life through art is art's sole justification, and through the chastening experience of a failed marriage why not look at another artist and his marriage? No reason at all – for this is precisely what Simon does in his next song, almost unique in his output with regard to most of its subject-matter, and recalling the 'Frank Lloyd Wright' song of *Bridge Over Troubled Water*. The title almost says it all: 'René and Georgette Magritte With Their Dog After the War', for that is what it is about. René Magritte was a great surrealist artist of the first half of the twentieth century, born in Belgium in 1898 and dying there in 1967. It is customary to talk of surrealist painters as if there was always a 'message' underlying their surrealism; occasionally there was, and sometimes close to the surface, but equally there often was not, and this enticing musical cameo is nothing more than what it says. The album sleeve is adorned (if that is the word) with a photograph (if you want to write a song about a face, said 'Song About the Moon' on side one, use a photograph – so here the artist, Simon, is following his own advice with a vengeance) of the couple, together with their dog, and

117

presumably after the war. The references to long-since forgotten harmony groups and bands of the 1930s adds a poigancy to the thought of this great artist and his wife alone, after the adventures of the day, listening to these old records, reminded of the past by glimpsing a display of clothes inspired by the period. The clothes in the morning, like the bodies of the lovers naked on the bed, are intertwined, once more recalling the imagery of those songs on the first side of the album.

This fascinating and beautiful little song, so slow and tender in tempo and in its human understanding comes almost as an Intermezzo in the proceedings before 'Cars Are Cars' picks up the travel theme of the 'Train In The Distance', song, and by so doing continues the ABAB nature of the album layout. It is a genuine fun song, as far as the lyrics are concerned, without any underlying seriousness, but the music occasionally disproves that. Indeed, the music is quite fascinating, being fast, as befits the subject, urgent and – as far as rock music is concerned, but unlike the vehicles – bouncy. To reinforce this – if one pardons the expression – driving rhythm Simon and Nile Rogers have programmed a Linn Drum Machine, which is laid down as the basis for the musical construction. Into their programming they have inserted milliseconds of silence (alluding to the use of a large slice of silence in 'Allergies' quite strongly, but here all over in a moment, like a constant vivid blink) which have created an extraordinarily apt and striking pulse. But the engine does not fire quite as smoothly as might be inferred, for the constant gaps of silence introduce a slightly tongue-in-cheek effect. The song, frankly, is not really up to much, but serves a pleasant enough purpose.

Travel, cars, motorcade, the deep south, imply a reference to President Kennedy; rock-and-roll, the personal crisis of the artist and the impact on his work, surrealist

118

or not, the ability to range over his life objectively, imply a personal reaction to some event; the passing of time, of human relationships, hearts and bones, imply death. All these strands are inextricably woven into the superb final song, a lament, ostensibly for 'The Late Great Johnny Ace', an early brilliant guitarist who died young, but transformed by the breathtaking range of literary allusion and by the most involved musical metamorphosis into a lament for all artists who die young, and more especially those who are killed by an assassin. The final verse reveals the impact of John Lennon's assassination on Simon, and this event, and the music which surrounds it, is taken by the composer Phillip Glass and transformed into a very moving *coda* to the entire album, scored for classical chamber orchestra conducted by Michael Riesman, summing up in this wholly remarkable statement a veritable wealth of influence. The end of *Sergeant Pepper* is recalled, and some of Simon and Garfunkel's earlier work, but the classical influences which we have noted in his work are also, because of the instruments involved, recalled in timbre and method, and the whole thing is capable of a variety of interpretation in the literary allusion of 'Johnny/Ace/Lennon', 'ace' in this context also equating with greatness. The musical allusions and metaphors, particularly the half-quotation from the Beatles' 'Yesterday' (played – without voices – by the strings, a clear reference to Paul McCartney's original versions), are immensely moving. But just at the point when one expects the album to fade into the distance, Simon cuts the music off, stops it, and we are left with silence – the sound of silence.

119

5   Art Garfunkel recordings 1973 to 1981

1973

ANGEL CLARE
For track listings see Discography p. 154

It is a fact of life that nothing is forever, and the separation of Simon and Garfunkel, although it dismayed their millions of fans and disappointed their record company, could have occurred at any time. Indeed, the fact they had been together for fifteen years was in itself unusual and possibly led people to think that they would, and could, go on for many years.

But relationships change, and we have touched upon the factors that led to their separation. By all accounts it was mutually satisfactory, without rancour, though one cannot imagine any separation to be entirely free of tension. In rock music changing personnel has been the order of the day, but one cannot have less than two in a group; when they change, everything changes, and when, as in Simon and Garfunkel's case, the people concerned were individually highly talented, their subsequent solo careers have to be seen as a continuation of their earlier work.

With Paul Simon the continuation is more apparent than with Art Garfunkel. Simon was the composer for the duo and was an outstanding instrumentalist; furthermore, he was the lyricist. It was possibly easier for him to pursue a solo career than for Garfunkel, but as has been hinted at earlier and will be touched upon again in the final chapter, Garfunkel's ideas on music and its presentation were too important to be discarded or left to wither and die. Garfunkel was also interested in pursuing an acting career; it is a pity this part of his life has not developed more fully, but no one can split himself into two. Simon was the first with a solo album but Garfunkel (at that time making his second film, *Carnal Knowledge*) followed a year later with *Angel Clare*.

It is easy, knowing that Garfunkel was not a composer, to dismiss his solo efforts as little more than a corollary to the main story. This would be a mistake, and an affront to a very talented singer, and anyone who sells a million copies of his first album within a year of its release cannot be lightly dismissed.

But the fact remains that Garfunkel is a singer first and last and his ideas on production and presentation – and in choice of material – were able to blossom fully alone, without having to seek approval from his erstwhile mate. In this regard, *Angel Clare* is much more of a breakaway from *Bridge Over Troubled Water* than was Simon's solo *Paul Simon* album. Freed from the constraints of working with a partner, Garfunkel's choice of material reflects his individuality. It is wide-ranging, sometimes breathtakingly so, and shot full of the most imaginative touches in its arrangements.

The first thing that one notices on playing the Garfunkel albums is that the backing – frequently of an orchestral nature – is much more expansive and wide than on any earlier Simon and Garfunkel track. 'Travelling Boy' by Paul Williams and Roger Nichols is the first track, and the title has some significance. He includes songs by Van Morrison ('I Shall Sing' – an excellent number, brilliantly performed) and Randy Newman ('Old Man' – the theme of age touched upon again), and traditional melodies ('Barbara Allen'). This last is possibly the weakest track on the album, for the essentially simple folk song is given a full treatment, perhaps rather more than on reflection Garfunkel would now consider suitable. But it is sung with such touching simplicity and genuine depth of feeling that any criticisms on this score (quite literally!) are silenced.

Of course, the separation was not quite total; Simon himself appears as one of the guitarists on the album, and Larry Knechtel, the pianist on *Bridge Over Troubled Water*, is here too. The recording engineer, Roy Halee, who had worked with Simon and Garfunkel since *Bookends*, was responsible for this album and is credited with being part producer. But a criticism that must be made is that Garfunkel's voice, as recorded, is not sufficiently detached from the backing fabric to take on the independent life it clearly demands. It is no doubt what was intended, but at times one has to strain to catch the words – which was surely not the intention.

An interesting sidelight on pop recording history is the fact that the recording was enormously expensive to complete; Clive Davis blanched at the bill – over $250,000 – but the sales amply justified the expenditure. Whether the artistic result would have been all that different if fewer location tracks had been undertaken is another question, and it is certainly true that in the chastened economic climate of the early 1980s a record company would not permit its artists to be quite so free with money in their pursuit of artistic satisfaction.

Furthermore, another historical point is the large poster given away with the album. This shows Garfunkel and presumably Halee in Grace Cathedral in front of a simple microphone set-up. This grained photograph adds nothing, of course, to our understanding or perception and is an example of that curious packaging kick which even the greatest artists indulged in at the time. So bad did this become with many bands that their music – and with it their message – was in grave danger of becoming submerged beneath an ecologically unacceptable pile of waste paper. As Maurice Oberstein, one of the world's great record men and a senior executive with CBS in London, caustically observed (not *à propos Angel Clare*), 'Are we in the music business or the print business?' – a sentiment that many music lovers would echo. But perhaps this phenomenon could be seen as an early run towards the use of visuals to promote music, which in the technologically superior late 1970s manifested itself in the video promotion film, to such an extent that 'popular' music could only, it seems, be conceived with a pictorial image that could be filmed to accompany it.

Imagine what a field day video promoters would have had if they had Simon's 'America' to work with; the images are all there waiting to be picked up, but there is no doubt that much would be lost in the process. The listener's imagination would not be allowed to work over the words, to picture his own scenes on the bus, and the occasionally brilliant video productions detract from our understanding of the music. This is not a criticism of video, merely a warning against its misuse, although in the early 1980s it is hard to lose the impression that much popular music today is almost operatic in conception, with the singers having to act out the songs as well as playing and singing them.

This may seem a far cry from *Angel Clare*, but Garfunkel is such an imaginative singer that the conclusions have to be drawn. Another most important development on this album is the inclusion of two songs by Jimmy Webb. Webb is one of the most important popular composers to have come out of America. He suffers little by comparison with Simon's literary imagery; witness Webb's classic 'MacArthur Park', a

124

surprising hit for the English actor, Richard Harris. Harris recorded two albums of Webb songs, one of which, *The Yard Went On Forever*, contains some sensational material. A theme running through Webb's work has been man's relationship with woman, and it is difficult not to avoid the impression that Webb is no lover of the feminist movement. His women are almost always two-faced, damaged or scheming, or – as in 'The Yard Went On Forever' song – used and put upon. Yet when they stand up for their rights, he is often less than sympathetic. 'All I Know', which begins side two, is the first Webb song, and 'Another Lullaby', which ends it, is the other. They are clearly very close to Garfunkel's heart, so closely does he sympathize with them.

1975

BREAKAWAY
For track listings see Discography p. 154

The second album, *Breakaway* , which followed in 1975, continues the processes a stage further. There is the same full orchestral backing, even if not quite as self-indulgent as on *Angel Clare*, and the same kind of presentation of splendid material. Richard Perry is the producer, but truth to tell the sound-image is hardly different from that on *Angel Clare*; indeed, the fault noted above, that Garfunkel's voice is not as detailed as it might be, is just as noticeable. With great daring, and ignoring the kind of criticism that he might have thought would be levelled at him, Garfunkel includes two old 'standards', 'When I Fall In Love, It Will Be Forever' (one of Nat King Cole's greatest recordings, and surprisingly resuscitated for Jimmy Osmond in 1973) and 'I Only Have Eyes For You', which was a monster hit for Garfunkel, reaching number one in Britain late in 1975 and staying in the

125

charts for eleven weeks. Also included on the album is the same recording as on Paul Simon's *Still Crazy After All These Years*, 'My Little Town' – surely a unique instance of the same track being issued on two albums by different artists. Although pressing quality may vary and albums may be recut, even though it is the identical recording, it sounds better on the Garfunkel album, than on Simon's. Perhaps it was remixed for this use, but the sound is cleaner and has a greater sense of stereo separation (but not too much, the essence has not been changed). In spite of the overall similar expression, and the inclusion of a galaxy of star guests (Graham Nash, David Crosby, Paul Simon himself of course, among others), this album does have a somewhat greater feeling of individuality, of detachment from the mainstream, than *Angel Clare*. One's only real regret is that space was not found for what could well be Garfunkel's greatest solo recording – the haunting song 'Second Avenue' of 1974, which was issued in the UK as a single. This is a truly great performance of a wonderful song, and it is a tragedy that it never made the charts, for it deserved to.

1978

WATERMARK
For track listings see Discography p. 155

With Garfunkel's third album, *Watermark* (1978), we encounter his first distinctive solo effort. Richard Perry is replaced by Garfunkel himself, aided by the brilliant keyboard player Barry Beckett as associate producer, and the difference in sound image and vocal separation from the first two albums is startling. This, one feels, is what should have been happening a long time ago. The separation and solo miking make Garfunkel take on an altogether different aspect. He starts, challengingly, with '(What A) Wonderful World', which is the Sam Cooke hit of 1960. Garfunkel is no black singer, but he rings the changes here with an exceptional piece of singing, free and floating, irresistible in its cumulative power and a thrilling start to what was arguably his best album up to that time. The album is completed with no less than eleven more Jimmy Webb songs, turning the disc into a showcase for Webb's exceptional songwriting craft.

Garfunkel includes a Richard Harris-recorded song, 'Watermark', but it is difficult to recognize the same song in this version. Harris – like Garfunkel – puts over the words with the understanding of an actor, making the song almost operatic in impact. But Garfunkel is by far the greater singer and his delineation of the tortuous melodic line is infinitely more musical and revealing. However, the searing intensity of Harris's performance has much to commend it – once heard, it can never be forgotten – and Garfunkel's approach is the emotional opposite. Harris is involved, Garfunkel the detached observer; both approaches are valid, but Garfunkel's has too great an air of detachment for words like 'I keep looking through old varnish at my late lover's body . . . and decaying . . . disappearing, even as I sing this song'. The ecstatic high instrumental line here is thrilling and one can only applaud Garfunkel's courage in taking this material and presenting it in such a flawless and fascinating manner.

The other unusual song on the album is not, strictly speaking, a Webb original, but an arrangement by him of an Irish folk-song, 'She Moved Through The Fair', recorded appropriately enough in Dublin with The Chieftains. One wishes it had been left at that, but regrettably the song is 'produced' with an unsuitable backing that destroys much of the earthy folkiness.

FATE FOR BREAKFAST –
DOUBT FOR DESSERT

For track listings see Discography p. 155

In 1979 Garfunkel's fourth solo album, *Fate For Breakfast – Doubt For Dessert* appeared, with yet another change of producer, this time to Louie Shelton (apart from the most successful track, 'Bright Eyes', which was recorded in London and produced by Mike Batt). The single of 'Bright Eyes' was Garfunkel's second number one hit in the UK and was the theme for the highly successful cartoon film – a full-length feature – of Richard Adams's classic children's book *Watership Down*. It is easy for rock enthusiasts to sneer at this, but it is a most beautiful song (composed by the enormously talented British musician Mike Batt, who has never quite received the recognition his undoubted great gifts deserve) and is sung to perfection. Whatever Garfunkel can or cannot do, he can sing, and he uses his naturally distinctive, pure and haunting voice admirably. Batt, an experienced producer as well as composer and performer, has moulded one of his finest tracks, and includes the rock guitarist, Chris Spedding (then soon to have a major hit with his own 'Motorbikin'') and the English classical oboist, composer and conductor Edwin Roxburgh (misspelled as 'Hoxburgh' on the sleeve credits). The remaining tracks are not really up to this standard, though they nearly are, and inhabit the same overall cushioned sound-world. The album could with profit have had rather more variety (a recurrent complaint against Garfunkel albums) but this is to miss the main point. While most people play an album straight through, one does not have to; one or two tracks at a time make this a splendid collection and one should not necessarily approach everything in the same way—though this comment could also be applied to the contents of the record in question.

1981

SCISSORS CUT
For track listings see Discography p. 155

In 1981 Art Garfunkel announced that his fifth solo album, *Scissors Cut*, would be his last. Following the pattern of most of the previous albums, Garfunkel includes some Jimmy Webb songs, and returns to Roy Halee for his swansong. The collection of material shows the greatest discrimination and fastidiousness in its choice and presentation, which is not surprising in view of the veritable galaxy of stars Garfunkel assembled to bid him goodbye; Simon is here, singing along with Garfunkel on Jimmy Webb's 'In Cars', which is a curious track. The singing is not up to their remembered standard, and the production probably has more hidden in it with aural innuendos than is apparent at a first, or even a fifteenth, hearing. It fades off, perhaps recalling the 'Homeward Bound' message, or even 'America', as though the journey is never ending, with a snatch of Bob Dylan's 'Girl From The North Country', and ends with the appropriately titled 'That's All I've Got To Say', as sure an indication of finality as 'Song For The Asking' is on *Bridge Over Troubled Water*. The digital recording is outstanding, and the album is cryptically dedicated to 'Bird'.

Thus does Garfunkel's recorded career as a solo artist come to an end, on his own admission, and it is unkind to claim, as many do, that in essence it meant very little. Garfunkel had great success early on in his solo career and we should be grateful to him for using his influence to showcase much fascinating material that would probably not have sold as well in other versions. His flexibility as an artist, always receptive to new ideas within his chosen framework, has produced some classic moments in popular music-making, and although it is unlikely that his solo career will in time come to be regarded very highly, it remains a fascinating appendix to the blazing career of Simon and Garfunkel.

6 Poet, Musician, Artist – *a critical commentary*

When ten million people buy a copy of the same album, it is safe to assume that it is a recording of some significance. The reverse is not necessarily true. While a great many unworthy albums manage to be released and deservedly do not sell, there are also a significant number of very worthwhile musical statements, sometimes great ones, which for one reason or another never get the chance of reaching a wide audience. If Simon and Garfunkel had issued twenty-one albums that sold in small quantities, the reason for such a book as this would be hard to seek: what significance, within a popular culture, can there be for something which is manifestly not popular? Only a handful of enthusiasts would be interested in pursuing the subject, though there have been instances where artists have had greater success after their death than when they were alive. Such instances are mercifully few, yet there is always an element of inverted snobbery that implies that something which is popular cannot possibly be worthwhile. The main body of this book – the detailed analyses of the recorded legacy to date of Paul Simon and Art Garfunkel – has attempted to show why we should investigate the phenonemon of this remarkable pair, and this concluding essay, divorced from the detailed discussion of each album, attempts to put their work into perspective.

It is as well to state now that the old widely held belief that popular music is essentially ephemeral and without lasting significance is no longer tenable. Since the advent of rock music in the mid 1950s, and the myriad developments it has spawned since then, the number of worthwhile artists has grown to such an extent that that old-fashioned view of popular music has to be discounted. If the music of early rock musicians was worthless, why is it that, getting on for (in some cases) thirty years after it first appeared it still retains the power to affect people, to move them in some way, to make them want to return again and again to the performance? If such music is indeed worthless, it would have disappeared along with the fashions of its day. The fact that it has not, and appeals anew to younger generations, conclusively proves that factors other than fashions are involved. Simon and Garfunkel, although they were impressionable teenagers when rock music began and, being American, were in the thick of the action, were influenced by early rock. They could hardly have remained untouched by it, if only by the circumstance of history.

This book began with a biographical outline that detailed the United States involvement in the Second World War. The war changed the Western world in many ways, not least in political and sociological ones. It was the last great conflict in our history, and it is to be hoped that it will remain so, but because it was so great, so wide-ranging in its effects, a whole generation of mankind was changed by it. When it was over, and victory for the Allies had been achieved, the cost in human and economic terms could only begin to be counted.

Popular culture, the entertainment of the masses, has always had an element of escapism about it. This is no recent phenomenon: it is the essence of popular art. Between the wars, with the economic climate of the world in tatters, the entertainment industry flourished. Millions flocked to what were termed 'picture palaces' — and palaces they were. Large, extravagant buildings with

132

fittings and decoration on a scale far removed from everyday life. The working class lived in dwellings that were barely adequate; their centres of mass entertainment, the cinemas and ballrooms, were literally palaces compared with their places of work and habitation.

For their escapism after the shocking experience of the Second World War people naturally turned in music to a style that offered aural balm and comfort from the rigours of postwar austerity. As America was at that time the richest nation on earth, whose civilian population had largely escaped the sufferings Europeans had endured, it may at first seem strange that such a movement as rock and roll should have started there. But it did not start in the affluent cities of the north. It began and grew from an essentially white, often deprived, working class, and a working class that, ten years after the cessation of hostilities, had begun to reject the established popular music. We know that each generation reacts against the previous one, if only to establish its own identity, and so such an event as the rock revolution should have been foreseen and expected; and for other reasons, too. It is a curious fact that movements in painting and literature often precede similar movements in music by several years. Just why music lags behind the other arts in this way is difficult to understand, but it does. As this is true in 'art' music, so it is in popular music. The archetypal rock and roll enthusiast has – by and large – always dressed in a certain way, but the D.A. hairstyle, with greased, high-combed hair, the leather truck driver's jacket, the jeans and chunky footwear, were already fashionable before Elvis Presley cut his first Sun single, as the Marlon Brando and James Dean films of 1951-4 show. This fashion was a rejection of ordered clothing, of conformity, of the standards of the older

133

generation. The juke-box music in these films, however, is an anachronism, being largely a kind of watered down big band jazz. The youth of the time had to wait several years before Elvis Presley's 'Hound Dog' and 'Heartbreak Hotel', but when it did arrive, it was clearly recognized for what it was.

It is often maintained that rock music became watered down and lost its drive at the end of the 1950s and the early 1960s, and that it was not until The Beatles that these qualities were regained. While this is plausible enough, up to a point, the fact remains that what we call the 'rock revolution' was not as complete as some would like to think. A glance at the charts at the time of Presley's early successes, for example, shows a wide range of music (far wider in technique and range than we encounter in the charts of the early 1980s) which also had followers, and this was not strictly rock music. What evolved from the fusion of what one might call ethnic rock and the then current 'Hit Parade' material was an attractive kind of popular music: music with a beat, but not wildly emphasized, based on rock rhythms, allied to a melodic strain, often harmonized, which clearly came from ballad singers. This music is cited as proof of the decline of rock, but it was a new fusion of its own, and produced some very fine records and highly talented musicians into the bargain. Of this kind, the Everly Brothers constitute a very good example.

They were intensely musical, very gifted, with distinctive voices that blended admirably. A whole succession of hits came from this duo, and they in turn influenced a great many other artists. The young Simon and Garfunkel, harbouring dreams of being a singing duo, could hardly fail to become influenced by the Everlys, and their early Big records show this influence almost to the exclusion of any other.

Simon learned the guitar as a child in the late 1940s; he and Garfunkel were intelligent and clever, both born into musical homes. With such a background, it is not surprising that they were familiar with a wide range of music and sympathetic to all styles, even as young teenagers. This breadth of sympathy was remarkable in early rock singers, who tended to plough one furrow, and to the elements of rock (transformed into a softer style by people such as the Everlys – although this 'softness' is one of degree: listen to their electrifying 'Claudette', which is great rock music) which caught the eager ears of Simon and Garfunkel should be added the purer sound of folk music. The folk group The Kingston Trio had a number one hit with 'Tom Dooley' (a genuine folk song) in 1958, and this created great interest in the folk idiom. It was yet another reaction: acoustic guitars, devoid of electronic blasting, are more basic, and infinitely more supple. This was the instrument Paul Simon played, and sang to: what could be more natural for the young singer-songwriter than to absorb elements of folk into his evolving style?

What is still missing from this is Simon's notable ingredient: literacy. What catalyst managed to bring out Simon's literary qualities? It was another singer-songwriter of broadly similar background – Bob Dylan. Dylan's influence on popular music has occasionally been overestimated, but it was wide and profound – exceptionally in his literary influence, far less for the musical. Dylan, like Simon – though Simon had less flamboyance – had remarkable gifts for verbal imagery of a truly poetic nature. Dylan's abrasive qualities and his primitive instrumentation (at least in the early days) are nowhere to be found in Simon's work, apart from the occasional suggestion in the earlier songs, but his literary skills must have struck a responsive chord in Simon's imagination.

It is the consistently high standard of Simon's work as a lyricist that is one of the most important aspects of his art. It is important, because whereas a tune can make itself felt at a first hearing the words, and their subtler implications, often do not. This view can be applied to any musical setting of words. It is only after a period of familiarity that the inner meanings of the poetry being set make themselves clearer. To some, it matters little about the words of a popular song; they claim – with some justification – that no one bought a record because of the words, for it was the music that attracted them in the first place. While this may be true, it is also right to point out that only with greater familiarity can the implications be explored.

To the two influences identified earlier, poetic imagery was the third main ingredient, and by 1963 Paul Simon had been exposed to them long enough for the synthesis with his own creativity to have become complete. As a performing musician he needed the contact and experience of live gigs. Unable to get work in New York, he travelled – somewhat surprisingly – to England, rather than going to look for America. By late 1963 London was becoming the swinging capital of the decade. The Beatles had had their early major successes and were on everyone's lips, being followed by a whole succession of British bands of the highest significance. London was 'where it was at', and it says much for Simon's strength of purpose that having chosen to go to England to live and work, performing and creating in such an exciting environment, his own art remained itself, utterly without influence from such groups. This is principally because Simon performed at folk clubs and pubs, away from the group venues. His art has always been more intimate, more personal, and yet the temptations to change his style must have been great.

Another influence, and one that soon was to become most important, was reuniting with Art Garfunkel. Garfunkel's background was similar to Simon's, but not being a performing musician himself he could bring a sympathetic yet detached view to any problems. Garfunkel's main contribution – and indeed the only one as far as the public was concerned – was his voice, so distinctive and memorable that his timbre is as much a part of those classic recordings as Simon's words and music. It is impossible to define exactly the influence one person has upon another, especially when they have known each other from the cradle, but in the light of Garfunkel's solo albums he must have contributed much in the creative process.

And so, by the time of their first success together, they had a combination of qualities that enabled them to withstand the rigours of pop music superstardom. The time was ripe for any success they were likely to achieve. Why then, was this combination – of Simon's songs and their expression within a distinctive vocal style – so successful at the time, and in what manner do these songs possess lasting qualities?

There are two main reasons for the first, apart from any inherent qualities the songs had. The first was that Simon and Garfunkel had the good luck to be signed to the most important record company of the time. CBS's connections were world-wide, and no sooner had a single showed signs of being a hit in one country than it was immediately available in others as part of the same organization. International pressure could be brought to bear very quickly, which is essential in the case of a film, released simultaneously in many countries, and the phenomenal success of *The Graduate* album bears witness to the organization at work. Apart from their worldwide connections, CBS also possessed the

137

advantage of being run by a very remarkable man, Clive Davis. Davis's tenure of the office of president was colourful and exciting, and during the time he ran the company a number of very important signings were made: apart from Simon and Garfunkel there were Janis Joplin, Chicago, Blood, Sweat and Tears, and The Byrds, among many others, and the combination of this impressive roster of the best of the new American bands and performers made the company the most significant in rock music at the time. They knew how to promote: the sampler albums *Rock Machine Turns You On* and *Rock Machine I Love You* opened up a whole new market for music that only a few years previously would have been regarded as almost impossible to sell.

Not that all the credit must go to Davis: the company was successful before he took over, and has gone from strength to strength since his unsavoury departure, but he symbolized the aggressive urgency that was brought to bear by the company in the market-place to get the music across to as wide an audience as possible. No other record company – not even EMI with The Beatles, or Decca with The Rolling Stones – had quite that burning commitment to music. At times CBS handled their product with an almost religious fervour, and without Davis at the helm at that time things might have been very different.

The second main reason is that Simon and Garfunkel offered a viable alternative to the proliferating rock bands of the time. Duos are by no means unknown, but at the time of the rise of Simon and Garfunkel, the Everly Brothers were on the wane. This is not to say that Simon and Garfunkel took their place but that there was no international competition for such a duo. This alternative meant that without a heavy drum section (in spite of Tom Wilson's efforts to the contrary) and the obligatory electric guitars, the sound of Simon and Garfunkel was quieter, calmer and altogether more subtly fashioned. They did not possess rock voices, and could no more shout the blues than an operatic soprano. Their voices were naturally quiet and even, so that no matter what song they sang – and their range was very wide – the song always stood the best possible chance. Subtle they may be, but they were not obtuse, and there was no mistaking the point being made.

To a society troubled by the growing US involvement in Vietnam, by the assassinations of that country's more enlightened leaders, by the upheaval of the black civil rights movement and its proliferating violence, by student unrest in Europe and in America, by the instability of seemingly secure European political institutions (particularly in France), and the Russian invasion of Czechoslovakia, the disillusionment by the realization that unchecked personal liberty (made easier by more liberal laws and the invention of the Pill) does nothing to curb aggression: in short, in a world that was going through a major upheaval as millions of babies born to the families of returning soldiers after the war were coming to maturity, the popular music of Simon and Garfunkel appeared above the din and hectic activity of everyday life, pointing towards more lasting values. The very titles of their hits, 'The Sounds Of Silence', 'Homeward Bound', 'Bridge Over Troubled Water', suggest this, and their detached sympathy for the helpless Mrs Robinson struck a responsive chord in the children of the generation of Mrs Robinson's own children, and in the millions of Mrs Robinsons. Their appeal was consequently wide and covered several generations. The reasons for their success were artistic quality and originality, at the right time, and offering a necessary alternative.

Having divined the influences and charted the progress, let us now examine their artistic qualities. The first thing that strikes the listener to the early Paul Simon songs (i.e. those written between 1963 and 1967) is their resemblance to folk song. Occasionally Simon took an existing song and turned it to his own purposes, but in so doing he often changed it – not out of all recognition but for his own purposes – and by so doing created a new and perhaps more relevant and worthwhile statement. This is nothing new in popular music, for singers invariably take material as a basis for their own interpretation, but Simon added new dimensions in changing the material to a virtually original creation. In classical music Handel, for example, was the master at taking other people's work and recomposing it to make it his own. His oratorio *Israel in Egypt* is possibly the best case of this, and the use of classical influences is another part of the Simon and Garfunkel mix. 'American Tune', although not strictly speaking a classical piece, as we have seen, falls into this category, but the prime example from their earlier work is 'Benedictus'. This was Garfunkel's most important public contribution, and he followed it on *Angel Clare* with another Bach adaptation. This interest in classical music extended to the use of classical instrumental timbre: harpsichord (essentially a baroque instrument) and oboe solos are not uncommon in Garfunkel's work, and occur in Simon's solo work as well. The result is that the listener's experience of sound is stretched, is intrigued by an instrument he is unlikely to encounter in rock music. In this regard, Simon and Garfunkel were not alone among their contemporaries: the Moody Blues used classically based orchestration to showcase their distinctive talents and were highly successful with it, and the classically trained Rick Wakeman was able to bring the same approach, albeit a more rock-oriented one, to his work. On the other side, David Bedford, the English composer and ex-rock musician, who played with Kevin Ayres and The Whole World, utilized his experience from both sides of the fence to create a fascinating sound-world in his later classical pieces, and Bedford's association with Mike Oldfield has done much to break down the unnecessary barriers that still exist between rock and classical music. These names are but a handful, chosen at random, from a veritable school of popular music of the late 1960s and early 1970s, but Simon and Garfunkel took what they needed from classical music and likewise turned it to good use.

Simon, being classed as a 'folk' singer at the start of his career (the *Wednesday Morning, 3 a.m.* album claims that the contents are 'exciting new sounds in the folk tradition' in a desperate attempt to express what the album contained, though 'folk' music, as it is generally understood, was but a small part of the album) was nevertheless able to use just what he wanted from folk music and no more, in the same way that he used other streams. 'Scarborough Fair' is the prime example of this, but as has already been demonstrated this too became virtually an original composition. From folk Simon took not only the contour of tunes and somewhat simple harmonies, but also the instrumental sounds. 'El Condor Pasa' is an excellent case: an original folk recording to which modern words have been added, to create anew a composition and a more relevant statement. Of course anyone can take existing material and play with it, but it takes a composer of genius – which I believe Paul Simon to be – to show us a new perspective and in the process create a distinctive and original work of art. It is almost the musical equivalent of the *objets trouvées* movement in pictorial art, and this was also mirrored in

141

contemporary classical music of the time. The *Sinfonia* by Luciano Berio, for example, a remarkable composition originally written for the Swingle Singers and the New York Philharmonic, uses the third movement from Mahler's Second Symphony as the basis for one of its own movements, superimposing above Mahler's music, which is played complete, a veritable collage of sounds and verbal patterns, like a hallucinatory dream.

Simon and Garfunkel had utilized a kind of musical collage for years before this: even the mixture of two songs on 'Scarborough Fair' shows this process at work, and the 'Voices of Old People' carries it to its extreme. It is significant that after this experiment, which is largely successful, Simon and Garfunkel never again returned to an album track that contained no music.

The later adoption of gospel procedures in Simon's work might be thought to be an extension of the awakening black consciousness movement in the America of the 1960s, and the growing international success of black groups and singers. Tamla Motown and the Philly Sound have already been mentioned, but gospel music is not just black music: it is religious music, and religious themes have been in Simon's work from the start. Indeed, it may be stretching the point, but it is possible to discern them in his latest work, 'Silent Eyes' and 'That's Why God Made The Movies', as well as in the earliest songs, 'Blessed', 'The Sounds Of Silence', 'A Church Is Burning' and others. The religious aspect of Simon's work has fascinated many people, and has even prompted a book. This can be overemphasized, and it is probably better to think of such references as essentially spiritual ones, divorced from everyday life but commenting upon it and raising wider implications.

The mention of the religious content of these songs

142

leads to Simon's literary gifts. They are considerable; he is a true poet. His lyrics run the whole gamut of literary devices, from alliteration to imagery. The very titles of the songs, from 'Sounds Of Silence' to 'Slip Slidin' Away' demonstrate this, but Simon must have been attracted by such alliteration in very early rock and roll: 'Good Golly, Miss Molly', 'I Ain't Sharin' Sharon', 'Lawdy Miss Clawdy', though in these cases the alliteration is manufactured. For Simon it is gentler, more subtle, but literate and expressive as well. He is fascinated by words, sometimes admitting that the more obscure imagery has arisen because he likes the sound of the word sequence, without giving too great a thought to their exact meaning. In this regard he has much in common with Gerard Manley Hopkins, whose line 'Glory be to God for dappled things' is echoed in the '59th Street Bridge Song' – 'I'm dappled and drowsy'. Apart from this, Simon's imagery is breathtaking. He possesses the enviable gift of creating a scene, of painting a picture, with a mere cluster of words, as in 'America', and 'Me And Julio Down By The Schoolyard', to take two examples from different periods of his art. It is a remarkable achievement, and one that would have ensured his immortality in popular music even if the music had been written by someone else.

But it is Simon's music, the expression of all the varied influences noted earlier, transformed into a personal yet fluently adaptable style, that has created the most immediate impression. A frequent criticism of his songs, at least in the earlier period, was that the harmonies which accompanied the singers were a little foursquare, somewhat too predictable. This is to complain that a leaf is green. Clearly, a folk-influenced writer will use those elements of folk music that he pleases, for in art anything is possible, given imagination and technical ability. As the message of the song, contained in the lyric, was of prime importance, it would have been stupid in the extreme to detract from the message by underpinning it with a whole succession of unrelated harmonies. Later on, as we have also seen, his harmonic thinking was given freer rein, until by the time of the *Still Crazy* album it had developed out of all recognition. But this is not the too-easy surprise of a style in which anything can happen: Simon's use of strange harmonies underlines the anguish of the songs concerned. Just as one cannot overload folk-oriented melodies with irrelevant harmonies, so one cannot express grief in a bland succession of major related chords: the expression demands a more fluid style.

In short Simon has moved with impressive consistency throughout his career. At no time does he appear uncertain about what he wants to express or how to express it. He is consistently sane in his approach, which does not preclude fantasy and vivid flights of imagination when they are called for. This personal integrity in just about his every song we have considered in this study is the most impressive of all his achievements.

Paul Simon's music is civilized in the best possible sense. He does not offend gratuitously, he is able to see both sides of a situation and express both with equal conviction. Running like a thread through these albums has been the duality of an emotion. Time and again one hears a song, is impressed by it, only to have it followed immediately by another song, completely different in its construction and expression, which on examination proves to be another aspect of the song which preceded it. This is a wholly original manner of composition, and although astrologers will claim this is because Simon is a Libran, and able to see both sides of a situation equally, it remains one of his most remarkable innovations in album layout.

If anything is possible in art, given the provisos

mentioned above, then at times it should be proved. The song 'So Long, Frank Lloyd Wright' is a classic example. Apparently Garfunkel, impressed by his friend's ability to write a song about almost any subject, suggested he write one on architecture. The result is a fascinating and wholly original creation, an object lesson in songwriting and final proof – if it were ever needed – of Simon's ability to do just that.

Above a pedal bass, like the deep foundations of a building, quietly insistent and permanent, strange disconnected chords prepare the entry of the singer. The chords fall in half steps, but because they are so close and yet so far, they have a tension that immediately connects with the curious. The first line 'So Long, Frank Lloyd Wright, I can't believe your song is gone so soon', is set to music in which the note values gradually get shorter until the last, which is the longest of the phrase. At this point the harmony falls to the major a third below, echoing the first two notes of the tune. By this simple device, a gentle oscillation of keys, Simon changes the image and perspective in readiness for the next phrase, which rises, passing through chromatic harmonies, almost like the musical personification of Wright's modern buildings. It soon becomes apparent, however, that Frank Lloyd Wright could be anyone, though the reference to 'architects may come and architects may go' brings us down to earth, containing with it a faint implication of 'architects = Art Garfunkel', set to the same note, constantly repeated over gently moving harmonies, like the permanence of a piece of architecture seen against the slow movement of the skies above and the motion of the earth below. 'I never laughed so long' is followed by 'so long', repeated irregularly like the intermittent waving of a railway passenger as the train slowly pulls out of the station and out of view. Against this, the harmonies again

145

move with impressive consistency, slowly, inexorably, like the passage of time, and all related to the tonic note that has been either heard or implied throughout the song, no matter how far away from it the passing melodies and harmonies seem to drift.

This song is by no means the best, and certainly not the most famous, on the *Bridge Over Troubled Water* album, but it is a remarkable achievement, not just by itself but in context: it comes at the end of side one, and fades into nothing, the 'so long' recalling the repeated 'ewig' (ever) at the end of Mahler's 'Song of the Earth'. The theme is of leaving, but leaving with a permanent memory ('we'd harmonize till dawn', 'when I run dry I stop awhile and think of you') and this must refer to Garfunkel and the planned separation.

What remains are the songs, and will remain so long as people retain the human qualities that can never fail to respond to them. These frequently flawless expressions of timeless human conditions and emotions, from birth to death, from tragedy to happiness, have been created during our lifetime by the genius of Paul Simon, perhaps the most wide-ranging and complete singer–songwriter of them all, a true 'child of our time' – but for all time.

Discography
Simon and Garfunkel albums

With the considerable quantity of recouplings, reissues and the custom packaging of many of the Simon and Garfunkel recordings, it has not proved possible to provide a fully detailed discography. This discography, therefore, concentrates on the albums in chronological order, following the text of the main body of the book. Singles, EPs, cassettes and 8-track editions are not included, apart from the few occasions when material has only appeared in such forms. The numbers are those of the UK releases: the assiduous collector should have no difficulty in tracing the record numbers for issues in his own particular territory.

There is a rough guide to the worth of each album: a record is awarded a number of stars (with a maximum of three) according to its importance. Detailed comment can, of course, be found under each album in the relevant chapter. When a record is listed without stars, it is considered to be generally unsatisfactory, although it may have the odd good track.

SIMON AND GARFUNKEL (Recorded as TOM AND JERRY)

Hey Schoolgirl; Our Song; That's My Story; Teenage Fool; Tia-juana Blues/Dancin' Wild; Don't say Goodbye; Two Teenagers; True Or False; Simon Says

Allegro 836 Recorded 1957-9. Released in UK 1967

WEDNESDAY MORNING, 3 A.M.

You Can Tell The World; Last Night I Had The Strangest Dream; Bleecker Street; Sparrow; Benedictus; The Sounds Of Silence/He Was My Brother; Peggy-O; Go Tell It On The Mountain; The Sun Is Burning; The Times They Are A-Changin'; Wednesday Morning, 3 a.m.

CBS 63370* Recorded 1964. Released in UK 1968

THE SOUNDS OF SILENCE

The Sounds of Silence; Leaves That Are Green; Blessed; Kathy's Song; Somewhere They Can't Find Me; Anji/ Homeward Bound; Richard Cory; A Most Peculiar Man; April Come She Will; We've Got A Groovey Thing Goin'; I Am A Rock

(The American issue of this album did not include 'Homeward Bound')

CBS 32020 (originally 62690)* Recorded 1965

PARSLEY, SAGE, ROSEMARY AND THYME

Scarborough Fair – Canticle; Patterns; Cloudy; The Big Bright Green Pleasure Machine; The 59th Street Bridge Song (Feelin' Groovy)/The Dangling Conversation; Flowers Never Bend With The Rainfall; A Simple Desultory Philippic (Or How I Was Robert McNamara'd Into Submission); For Emily, Whenever I May Find Her; A Poem On The Underground Wall; 7 o'Clock News – Silent Night

(The American issue of this album included 'Homeward Bound')

CBS 62860*** Recorded 1966

148

BOOKENDS

Bookends Theme; Save The Life Of My Child; America; Overs; Voices Of Old People; Old Friends; Bookends Theme/ Fakin' It; Punky's Dilemma; Mrs Robinson; A Hazy Shade Of Winter; At The Zoo

CBS 63101*** Recorded 1967/1968

THE GRADUATE

Songs performed by Simon and Garfunkel: The Sounds Of Silence; April Come She Will; Scarborough Fair – Canticle; The Big Bright Green Pleasure Machine; Mrs Robinson *Additional music composed and conducted by David Grusin:* The singleman Party Foxtrot; Sunporch Cha-Cha-Cha; On The Strip; The Folks; A Great Effect; Whew

CBS 70042 Recorded 1967

BRIDGE OVER TROUBLED WATER

Bridge Over Troubled Water; El Condor Pasa (If I Could); Cecilia; Keep The Customer Satisfied; So Long, Frank Lloyd Wright/The Boxer; Baby Driver; The Only Living Boy In New York; Why Don't You Write Me; Bye Bye Love; Song For The Asking

CBS 63699*** Recorded 1969

SIMON AND GARFUNKEL'S GREATEST HITS

Mrs Robinson; For Emily, Whenever I May Find Her; The Boxer; The 59th Street Bridge Song (Feelin' Groovy); The Sounds Of Silence; I Am A Rock; Scarborough Fair – Canticle/ Homeward Bound; Bridge Over Troubled Water; America; Kathy's Song; El Condor Pasa (If I Could); Bookends; Cecilia

CBS 69003*** Compiled 1972

149

THE SIMON AND GARFUNKEL COLLECTION

I Am A Rock; Homeward Bound; America; The 59th Street Bridge Song (Feelin' Groovy); Wednesday Morning, 3 a.m.; El Condor Pasa (If I Could); At The Zoo; Scarborough Fair — Canticle; The Boxer/The Sounds Of Silence; Mrs Robinson; Keep The Customer Satisfied; Song For The Asking; Hazy Shade Of Winter; Cecilia; Old Friends; Bookends Theme; Bridge Over Troubled Water

CBS 10029*** Compiled 1981

SIMON AND GARFUNKEL – THE CONCERT IN CENTRAL PARK, 19 SEPTEMBER 1981

Mrs Robinson; Homeward Bound; America; Me And Julio Down By The Schoolyard; Scarborough Fair/April Come She Will; Wake Up Little Susie; Still Crazy After All These Years; American Tune; Late In The Evening/Slip Slidin' Away; A Heart In New York; Kodachrome-Mabellene; Bridge Over Troubled Water/Fifty Ways To Leave Your Lover; The Boxer; Old Friends; The 59th Street Bridge Song (Feelin' Groovy); The Sounds Of Silence

Geffen Records GEF 96008 (2 record set)*

Simon and Garfunkel singles

Tracks not subsequently issued on albums

South/Golden Wildwood Flower

Recorded by Simon and Garfunkel as Tom and Jerry

Mercury 71753

I'm Lonesome/Lookin' At You

Recorded by Simon and Garfunkel as Tom and Jerry

Ember E 1094 (UK issue: Pye International 7N25202)

You Don't Know Where Your Interest Lies/Fakin' It

You Don't Know was never issued on a subsequent album; the take of Fakin' It is not the same as that issued on the 'Bookends' album

CBS 2911

Paul Simon solo albums

THE PAUL SIMON SONGBOOK

I Am A Rock; Leaves That Are Green; A Church Is Burning; April Come She Will; The Sounds Of Silence; A Most Peculiar Man/He Was My Brother; Kathy's Song; The Side Of A Hill; A Simple Desultory Philippic; Flowers Never Bend With The Rainfall; Patterns

CBS 62579*** Recorded 1965

151

PAUL SIMON

Mother And Child Reunion; Duncan; Everything Put Together Falls Apart; Run That Body Down; Armistice Day/ Me And Julio Down By The Schoolyard; Peace Like A River; Papa Hobo; Hobo's Blues; Paranoia Blues; Congratulations

CBS 69007*** Recorded 1971

THERE GOES RHYMIN' SIMON

Kodachrome; Tenderness; Take Me To The Mardi Gras; Something So Right; One Man's Ceiling Is Another Man's Floor/American Tune; Was A Sunny Day; Learn How To Fall; St Judy's Comet; Loves Me Like A Rock

CBS 69035*** Recorded 1972

LIVE RHYMIN'

Me And Julio Down By The Schoolyard; Homeward Bound; American Tune; El Condor Pasa (If I Could); Duncan; The Boxer/Mother And Child Reunion; The Sounds Of Silence; Jesus Is The Answer; Bridge Over Troubled Water; Loves Me Like A Rock; America

CBS 69059** Recorded mainly 1973

STILL CRAZY AFTER ALL THESE YEARS

Still Crazy After All These Years; My Little Town (with Art Garfunkel); I Do It For Your Love; 50 Ways To Leave Your Lover; Night Game/Gone At Last; Some Folks' Lives Roll Easy; Have A Good Time; You're Kind; Silent Eyes

CBS 86001** Recorded 1975

GREATEST HITS, ETC.

Slip Slidin' Away; Stranded In A Limousine; Still Crazy After All These Years; Have A Good Time; Duncan; Me And Julio Down By The Schoolyard; Something So Right/Kodachrome; I Do It For Your Love; 50 Ways To Leave Your Lover; American Tune; Mother and Child Reunion; Loves Me Like A Rock; Take Me To The Mardi Gras

CBS 10007** Recorded 1977 (first two tracks), remainder various dates (from previous albums)

ONE-TRICK PONY

Late In The Evening; That's Why God Made The Movies; One-Trick Pony; How The Heart Approaches What It Yearns; Oh, Marion/Ace In The Hole; Nobody; Jonah; God Bless The Absentee; Long, Long Day

Warner Bros K56846 Recorded 1980

HEARTS AND BONES

Allergies; Hearts and Bones; When Numbers Get Serious; Think Too Much (b); Song About The Moon/Think Too Much (a); Train In The Distance; Réne and Georgette Magritte With Their Dog After The War; Cars Are Cars; The Late Great Johnny Ace.

Warner Bros 92-3942-1*** Recorded 1981, 1982, 1983

Paul Simon singles

Tracks not subsequently issued on albums

He Was My Brother/Carlos Dominguez

Recorded by Paul Simon as Jerry Landis; both written by Simon and never reissued

Oriole CB 1930 Recorded c. 1964

Art Garfunkel solo albums

ANGEL CLARE

Travelling Boy; Down In The Willow Garden; I Shall Sing; Old Man; Feuilles-Oh; Do Space Men Pass Dead Souls On Their Way To The Moon?/All I Know; Mary Was An Only Child; Woyaya; Barbara Allen; Another Lullaby

CBS 69021* Recorded 1972

BREAKAWAY

I Believe (When I Fall In Love, It Will Be Forever); Rag Doll; Break Away; Disney Girls; Waters Of March/My Little Town (with Paul Simon); I Only Have Eyes For You; Lookin' For The Right One; 99 Miles From L.A.; The Same Old Tears On A New Background

CBS 86002* Recorded 1974

WATERMARK

Crying In My Sleep; Marionette; Shine It On Me; Watermark; Saturday Suit; All My Love's Laughter/(What A) Wonderful World; Mr Shuck 'n' Jive; Paper Chase; She Moved Through The Fair; Someone Else (1958); Wooden Planes

CBS 86054* Recorded 1976/1977

FATE FOR BREAKFAST – DOUBT FOR DESSERT

In A Little While (I'll Be On My Way); Since I Don't Have You; All I Know; Sail On A Rainbow; Miss You Nights/Bright Eyes; Finally Found A Reason; Beyond The Tears; Oh How Happy; When Someone Doesn't Want You; Take Me Away

CBS 86082* Recorded 1979

SCISSORS CUT

Scissors Cut; A Heart In New York; Up In The World; Hang On In; So Easy To Begin/Can't Turn My Heart Away; The French Waltz; The Romance; In Cars; That's All I've Got To Say

CBS 85259* Recorded 1981

Art Garfunkel singles

Second Avenue/Woyoya

CBS 2672 Recorded 1972/1974

We Are Going/Second Avenue
CBS 4778† Recorded 1974/1976

Second Avenue and We Are Going have never been issued in album form.

Filmography

THE GRADUATE

An Embassy Production, distributed by United Artists
Filmed in Panavision Technicolor

Starring Dustin Hoffman, Anne Bancroft, Katherine Ross, Murray Hamilton, William Daniels, Elizabeth Wilson

Producer .... Lawrence Turman
Director .... Mike Nichols
Photographer .... Robert Surtees

Songs Mrs Robinson; The Sounds Of Silence; April Come She Will; Scarborough Fair – Canticle; The Big Bright Green Pleasure Machine. Sung by Simon and Garfunkel

Additional music composed and conducted by David Grusin

105 minutes

1970

CATCH 22

Paramount Studios
Filmed in Panavision Technicolor

Starring Art Garfunkel, Alan Arkin, Martin Balsam, Richard Benjamin, Jack Gilford, Buck Henry, Bob Newhart, Anthony Perkins, Paula Prentiss, Jon Voight, Martin Sheen, Orson Welles

Producer ....John Calley, Martin Ranschoff
Director ....Mike Nichols
Photographer ....David Watkin

No music used in the film

122 minutes

1971

CARNAL KNOWLEDGE

An Icarus Production
Filmed in Panavision Technicolor

Starring Arthur Garfunkel, Jack Nicholson, Candice Bergen, Ann-Margret, Rita Moreno

Producer/Director ....Mike Nichols
Photographer ....Guiseppe Rotunno

Songs by various artists

97 minutes

1975

SHAMPOO

A Vista Production
Technicolor

Starring Warren Beatty, Julie Christie, Lee Grant, Goldie Hawn, Jack Warden, Tony Bill

Producer .... Warren Beatty
Director .... Hal Ashby
Photographer .... Laszlo Kovacs

Music by Paul Simon

110 minutes

1977

ANNIE HALL

United Artists
Color by De Luxe

Starring Woody Allen, Diane Keaton, Tony Roberts, Carol Kant, Paul Simon, Shelly Durall

Producer .... Jack Rollins/Charles H. Joffe
Director .... Woody Allen
Photographer .... Gordon Willis

Music: Various

93 minutes

1980

BAD TIMING

Rank/Recorded Picture Company
Technovision

Starring Arthur Garfunkel, Theresa Russell, Hervey Keitel, Denholm Elliott, Daniel Massey

Producer .... Jeremy Thomas
Director .... Nicholas Roeg
Photographer .... Guiseppe Rotunno

Music by Richard Hartley

123 minutes

1980

ONE-TRICK PONY

Warner Brothers
Technicolor

Starring Paul Simon, Blair Brown, Lou Reed, Tiny Tim

Producers .... Michael Tanner,
                                          Michael Hansman
Director .... Robert M. Young
Photographer .... Richard Bush

Music by Paul Simon

Songs: Late In The Evening; That's Why God Made The Movies; One-Trick Pony; How The Heart Approaches What It Yearns; Oh, Marion; Ace In The Hole; Nobody; Jonah; God Bless The Absentee; Long, Long Day

118 minutes

Bibliography

Bookends: The Simon and Garfunkel Story
  by Patrick Humphries, London 1981

Paul Simon: Now and Then
  by Spencer Leigh, Liverpool 1973

The Songs of Paul Simon
  London 1975

The Paul Simon Complete
  London n.d. 1980?

Inside the Record Business
  by Clive Davis, London 1975

Index of Song Titles

162

163

Index of Persons

165